Interview Preparation

How to Stand Out From the Crowd and Land Your
First Job

(Practical Job Interview Skills to Master Body
Language That Prepare for Ultimate Success in
Job Interviews)

George Young

Published by Rob Miles

George Young

All Rights Reserved

Interview Preparation: How to Stand Out From the Crowd and Land Your First Job (Practical Job Interview Skills to Master Body Language That Prepare for Ultimate Success in Job Interviews)

ISBN 978-1-989990-74-2

Legal & Disclaimer

The information contained in this book is not designed to replace or take the place of any form of medicine or professional medical advice. The information in this book has been provided for educational and entertainment purposes only.

The information contained in this book has been compiled from sources deemed reliable, and it is accurate to the best of the Author's knowledge; however, the Author cannot guarantee its accuracy and validity and cannot be held liable for any errors or omissions. Changes are periodically made to this book. You must consult your doctor or get professional medical advice before using any of the suggested remedies, techniques, or information in this book.

Upon using the information contained in this book, you agree to hold harmless the Author from and against any damages, costs, and expenses, including any legal fees potentially resulting from the application of any of the information provided by this guide. This disclaimer applies to any damages or injury caused by the use and application, whether directly or indirectly, of any advice or information presented, whether for breach of contract, tort, negligence, personal injury, criminal intent, or under any other cause of action.

You agree to accept all risks of using the information presented inside this book. You need to consult a professional medical practitioner in order to ensure you are both able and healthy enough to participate in this program.

Table of Contents

Introduction

Your job hunt has turned into an expedition riddled with hopelessness, and you are increasingly getting worried that you will never be employed. You have been lucky enough to secure an interview every time you have submitted an application for a job opening. However, your worry is that no job interview has ever gone in your favor. You are still unemployed. The joy that comes with getting hired is always life changing, but how many people have had this wish without it every seeing the light of day? If you are among those wishing for that big day, then you should ask yourself this question: what has always disqualified you from employment opportunities? Why is it that you have never succeeded at persuading an interviewing panel despite your good qualifications? It is commonly agreed that always being shortlisted for a job interview but failing to annihilate your competitors by crushing the interview is very worrying. There are a number of issues that could lead to this trend. It could be that you seem disinterested in the job because you do not always have the right information relating to the job or the hiring company. Another cause could be that you are ill prepared for an interview, which could mean that you are overconfident or that you didn't rehearse enough for the big day. There are also some people who, despite being shortlisted for a job interview, have always had their hopes crushed by poor communication skills. They simply can't persuade a panel, and this comes down to the manner in which they respond to questions. Further, failing to crush a job interview could be attributed to the problem of talking too much at the expense of listening properly to the questions being asked. This is irritating and is sure to cost you the job opportunity. Further, failing to secure a job after an interview could be attributed to other weaknesses on your side, such as not being persuasive when giving answers to interview questions. A poorly presented resume and facing an interview panel as a job beggar rather than as a human resource that is eager to make a change in the hiring organization are also some factors that will easily cost you a job opportunity. Many people who have failed to secure a job did so because they suffer from all these weaknesses with little knowledge about it.

In Chapter One, we will start with one of the most crucial elements for an interviewee to keep in mind before walking into the job interview. It is all about boosting your chances by taking things a notch higher when preparing for a job interview. We will also find out in Chapter One what makes information so powerful no matter where it is applied.

Chapter 1: Preparing Your Job Application

First thing's first. You have to get the interview. The two universal necessities of a job application process for basically any position are your CV/resume and cover letter. These two documents are your key to demonstrating why you deserve the opportunity to be considered for the role being offered. So before you can nail the interview, you need to focus on nailing these two pieces of information.

Your resume is like a passport showing all your past experiences and skills that will benefit you in the working world. Your resume should include all of the following: your past education, work experience, employment skills, personal attributes, achievements, qualifications, community involvement, interests and some referees.

The underlying theme your resume should follow is relevance. Avoid having a stock standard resume to use for each and every job you apply for. Try to include only what you can justify to interviewers as beneficial to your future in the position you're applying for if questioned on it. Don't be too restrictive with this, as I'll explain later how you can basically translate any past life experience into positive job experience, but try not to list your grade five paperboy job if going for a chief engineering role.

As far as layout is concerned, go for clear and concise. Whoever is reviewing your CV will likely be reviewing hundreds of others, so while you want yours to stand out in this sense, don't make it confusing. The best bet is to use a CV template, which you can easily download from the internet. You don't have to use bright colors or crazy fonts to grab their attention: using clear colors and matching fonts will work much better for you. Ensure that all of your contact details are included in your resume, have a final check for grammatical errors and try to keep everything to two or three pages in length - having a ten page long CV doesn't show that you're experienced; it shows that you can't summarize.

In addition to a sound CV, a cover letter must be included which states both why you're applying for the job and why you'd be the perfect candidate. Again, if you're really unfamiliar with the process, templates do exist on the internet, but the basic structure of your cover letter should be:

- Explain the purpose of your application and the role you're applying for

- Summarize your experience, skills and abilities that make you the ideal worker for this role

- State what drew you to this company/organization in particular, and how your personal attributes are in line with those of the company

- Conclude by thanking them immensely for considering your application, as well as mentioning any attachments such as your resume, recommendations from past employers and anything else they've requested to be included with your application.

It is even more important to customize your cover letter to the employer than it is to customize your CV; so don't try cutting, copying and pasting - write it from scratch! If the HR manager reviewing your cover letter gets the same stock standard paragraphs as the hundred others, it is likely to be discarded. Show that you are unique and also completely capable. The aim of a cover letter is to emphasize that you will be able to fulfill the roll, that you'll provide value for them (not the other way around) and that you're reliable. Be sure to include your contact details and limit your cover letter to a single page.

The last thing I want to make abundantly clear before you submit your job application is to make your social networking profiles bulletproof. This primarily includes Facebook and LinkedIn. With modern technology all it takes is a quick Google search from your potential future employer to find your Facebook profile picture which displays you chugging a jug of beer, and immediately toss your application in the trash. For Facebook ensure there is nothing condemning (especially incriminating) that can be viewed from a public search. The easiest way to do this is to set all of your pictures, posts and details to private, and ensure you have a respectable profile and cover photo.

Your LinkedIn profile is very important as well, as this can be publicly viewed in its entirety and an employer is very likely to at the least scan through it. Therefore you must make sure that you again have a respectable profile picture (no profile picture at all looks very bad), list all your relevant past work experience and a succinct description of yourself. You can think of this is an addition to, or verification of, your personal resume.

If you are subscribed to any additional social networking sites, be sure to check that they are air tight as well. If you can, find someone who is not already a friend or follower of yours to view your profiles through their own accounts to see exactly what information they can view, so you can check that your privacy settings are working as they should. A great final check once this is done is to do a Google search for yourself and see what comes up. If anything else appears which may look suspicious or questionable to employers, do your best to remove it completely.

Chapter 2: What to Wear

It doesn't matter if you're interviewing for a position as a mechanic or a call center manager, you should put some effort into your clothing. Business casual attire is appropriate for most interviews. That being said, if you're interviewing for higher level management position, or at a business where more formal attire is worn, such as at a law firm or political establishment, then Business Informal attire is the way to go. So let's distinguish between the two.

Business Casual is neat and professional, more formal than Smart Casual attire, but less formal than Business Informal attire. Confused yet? It is pretty vague, as there is no agreed upon definition for the style. Think Khaki pants, skirts, and slacks, as well as blouses, polo shirts, long sleeved shirts and sweaters. Darker or neutral colors are usually best. You want to stand out for your professional appearance, not for flashy colors. Business Casual is NOT runners, sweatshirts, or jeans.

Business Informal is a step up from Business Casual. Think slacks with a long sleeved button down shirt and a tie. You can skip the matching jacket, you don't need to wear a full suit – that would be Business Formal. For women a skirt with matching blazer and a button down blouse would go well here.

If you're still confused on the difference do a simple Google Image search for both terms. You will see tons of pictures to give you some clothing inspiration. When in doubt, ask someone! Ask your parents, your neighbor, or your best friend, "Does this look professional enough for my job interview"?

Remember, the goal is to look professional regardless of the position. First impressions will make or break you.

Common Interview Questions and Answers

You could literally spend days reading books with every kind of interview questions and appropriate answers for each. At this point you don't have time for that and you wouldn't be able to memorize it all anyway. That won't prepare you, and even worse, you'll lose focus on what is important. So this section is dedicated to the **most common** interview questions or variations of them with tips on how to answer. This list is not exhaustive but rather a guide to get you thinking of what you might say based on YOUR experience and how it relates to the job you're interviewing for.

Tell me about yourself. This is where you sum up your work history, any career accomplishments, and what brought you to this point of applying for this job. This should take you about 30 second. You don't need to go on and on about your life. It's ok to mention non-work related things like your hobbies or key personality traits but don't get too sidetracked.

For example, "After graduating from school I took a job with XYZ Company as a Salesperson. After 5 years I realized one of my biggest strengths was managing people so I moved on to ABC Company to be their manager. I have been working there, learning the ins and outs associated with the retail industry. Now, I'm looking for a bigger challenge, which is why I applied to this job. I think this type of working environment would suit me very well.

What are your career goals? Where do you see yourself in 2, 5, 10 years? You might say that you see yourself working your way up through a company, learning all aspects, to eventually be a manager. You might say you see yourself owning your own business. You should be open here about your career goals but don't make it sound like this job is just a pit stop on your way to someplace else.

What are your strengths? Some good strengths are communication, time management, diffusing difficult situations, sales or customer service, problem solving abilities, and computer skills. There are a lot of strengths and you have *at least* one. Own it and don't be afraid to brag, just a little. Be prepared to give an example of using that strength, in the workplace if possible.

What are your weaknesses? The trick here is to spin your answer to make the interviewer understand that you're pro-actively working on getting better. A couple of weaknesses to get you thinking might be your organization skills, your follow up after completing a task, or your time management. The employer wants to know what your weakness is so that they know how to manage or help you. For example, "My time management is my weakness but I make sure to put appointments and tasks into my calendar. The calendar reminders keep me focused and on task." You can see in this example the weakness and the action being taken to fix it.

Why are you leaving your current job? Do NOT say bad things about your current employer. It will give them a clear picture of how you will speak about them in the future if they hire you. It's ok to say that you're looking for a greater challenge, or there is no further opportunities for career growth where you are at, or the company culture isn't right for you. Keep it about YOURSELF! They don't want to hear all the terrible things you hate about the company or that your boss is a jerk. This is a big mistake that a lot of people make in an interview and it pretty much seals their fate of not getting hired. Even if you did have a negative experience, spin your answer to make it clear that you're excited for new opportunities.

How do you handle conflict with coworkers or customers? It's best to say that you rarely have conflict with others but you are aware that a process should be followed and it usually involves talking it through with your co-worker and then taking it your supervisor if a resolution can't be found on your own.

What accomplishments are you most proud of? You want to stick to work, school, or volunteer related subjects here. Don't say your kids.

Tell me about a difficult experience you've had while at work, and how you dealt with it. **Be specific, but brief. They want to**

hear <u>the potential problem, how you responded, and what the resolution was.</u>

What do you know about our company? This might actually be a question they ask you at the very start of the interview. DO YOUR RESEARCH. The worst thing you can say is that you don't know. Find out what they do/make, who they serve, where their other locations are (if any), and if they are involved in the community. You don't need to recite their company history but they are looking to see how great your interest in the job actually is so do your research. TIP: All of this information is likely on their website!

Why did you decide to apply for this position? Hopefully there is something compelling that made you apply, other than to earn a paycheck. If you don't have any experience in the field that you're applying to and you absolutely don't have a reason, just say that you applied for the position to gain experience in that specific field of work.

Why should we choose you? This is one you should think long and hard about before the interview. Just like the "Tell me about yourself" question. You should rehearse it and memorize it. Talk about your strengths and what you have to offer to the employer. Even if you have no experience with this particular job, *you still have something to offer*, whether it be your ability to learn quickly and adapt, your passion for that particular field, or a strong desire to learn!

What are you looking for in your ideal job or employer? Your answer should be in line with the job for which you are applying. You don't want to say you're looking for a work from home job when the job you are applying to is in a warehouse! A very safe answer would sound something like this: "I'm looking for an environment where communication is a top priority."

Chapter 3: How To Stay Cool Under Pressure And Build Your Self-Confidence

Confidence is the single most important element you can use to impress and charm anyone. This is quite true especially when it comes to acing job interviews. If you are not confident when answering questions asked by your interviewers or when addressing them, you are likely to come off as an unconfident, weak, and unimpressive person.

Even if you are highly talented, if you cannot convince your interviewers of your amazing abilities, you won't impress them or land the job. To ensure that does not happen, you need to communicate effectively, something that cannot happen if you're not confident and know how to stay calm under pressure.

Here are some tips to help build your confidence to make ensure you give a striking interview and create a great first impression on your interviewers.

Step 1: Improve Your Body Language

Your body language plays an important role in shaping your confidence and is an important aspect of your nonverbal communication. If you walk into a job interview slouched shoulders and arms crossed, you're likely to come off as an unconfident individual who is not sure of himself. You are quite likely to think the same of anyone who displays similar body language.

According to research by Harvard researcher Amy Cuddy, your body language is an important determinant of your confidence and stress levels. Her research shows that high power body language (wherein you keep your head held high, keep your shoulders and chest broad and open, keep your limbs open, and maintain direct eye contact with others) increases the testosterone levels in your body and decreases the cortisol levels.

On the other hand, low power body language (wherein you keep your head low, keep your shoulders and chest closed and slouched, keep your limbs crossed and do not maintain direct eye contact with others) does the opposite of that.

Testosterone is a hormone associated with confidence, poise, and enthusiasm whereas cortisol relates to increased stress and a lack of confidence. This shows that a high power body language helps increase your confidence levels and reduces your stress levels whereas a low power body language does the opposite of that. If you practice a high power body language, you are likely to feel confident and walk into the job interview with poise, which will help you create a good first impression.

To practice a high power body language, do the following:

Always stand straight with your chest and hips open.

Keep your shoulders broad, open, and never slouch.

Never cross your arms over your chest as this reflects a lack of confidence and frustration; always keep your arms to your sides.

Keep your legs slightly open when sitting, standing, or walking.

Maintain direct eye contact with your interviewers but keep your contact gentle instead of intimidating.

Work on these tips a little before your job interview and you will find yourself feeling more confident.

Step 2: Practice

Before the big day, practice answering all the questions you anticipate a few times so you can answer them fluently on the interview day. Make sure to rehearse the part where you want to convince the interviewers why they must hire you. If possible, speak in front of one or more people so they can pinpoint any of your flaws and help you correct them on time.

Step 3: Visualize

The more you believe in yourself and your abilities, the more confident you will feel about yourself. An effective way to increase your positivity and confidence is to practice visualization. When you visualize feeling confident in front of your interviewers and speaking confidently, strongly, and charismatically, you will start feeling good about yourself. This feeling will enhance your enthusiasm and self-belief, thus allowing you to give a fantastic interview.

To reap the benefits of visualization, visualize yourself walking into the interview room with confidence, speaking calmly and confidently with your interviewers, and voicing the right replies to all the questions. Imagine the interviewers looking at you happily and having charmed them with your charisma.

Add details to this visualization by adding in expressions, colors, sounds, and emotions. Start doing this a few days prior to your interview and do it on the day of the interview. By the day of the interview, you will feel extremely confident of your abilities.

In addition, draw a few deep breaths right before your interview to calm your stressed nerves. Deep breathing and visualization are both great ways to increase your confidence and sense of calmness so you can do anything you want successfully. While you work on all these techniques, incorporate the ones in the following section to ensure you get the job you want.

Chapter 4: The Q and A Segment

A huge part of the preparation is getting ready in answering interview questions. However, since you are not fully aware of what the exact questions are, you can still prepare yourself by practicing with the "most possible" questions that might be asked. Here are some of the possible questions you will most likely be asked and how you should answer them.

Question #1: Tell me something about yourself.

What the interviewer actually wants to know: **Who are you as a professional?**

Ideal Way to Answer: While it is tempting to talk about your hobbies, talents, personality, family or your childhood, this is not the best time to do so. What you should do is to give an overview of your skills and where you are right now in terms of your career.

Question # 2: Why are you interested in this job?

What the interviewer actually wants to know: Why you think this job is right for you? Is this the path you really want to take career-wise? Do you have the motivation and drive to stay in this job or this is just something to pass the time for you?

Ideal Way to Answer: Refer to the interesting points of the role, how you can help the company grow, and how it will contribute to your growth in the field. The interviewers pay attention to your enthusiasm and would want to hire someone who will be happy at the post every day. Talk about the salary, benefits, bragging rights and other small things could show that you are not really interested in the work itself – this will turn off the interviewer.

Question #3: Why did you leave your last job?

What the interviewer actually wants to know: Your weaknesses, your problem-solving skills, and your moral compass.

Ideal Way to Answer: This one can be a tricky one, especially if the reason for leaving is quite negative. If you left your job to seek new challenges, that's an appropriate thing to say. Of course, you have to back it up with something that this job you are eyeing has that the previous one did not. However, if you left because of office conflict, do not mention that. Do not complain or badmouth your former employers or co-workers. This will imply that you may have poor interpersonal skills, cannot stand up for yourself, easily aggravated, etc. You can simply say that your values or priorities have changed, and they do not match the previous company's anymore. It's okay if you'd to cite moving to a new location or financial instability of the other company.

It is important to remember that whatever you can (and might) be verified as the application process goes along. Therefore, you can stick to the facts but soften the blow for those touchy, negative feelings you may have about your former workplace.

Question #4: Why are you a good fit for this job?

What the interviewer actually wants to know: What are your strengths? What can you offer the company?

Ideal Way to Answer: This is one question you should really be prepared for because it is all about your skills, talents and all other qualifications that the job requires. Of course, you should have read the job description before you actually sent your resume for the job. Therefore, your task now is to match your strengths with those roles that the job entails. Talk about the jobs you did before if those are relevant in the job you are applying for now. Experience is always a plus. Highlight your abilities that be hard to find in other candidates too. Keep in mind – this is your time to shine! Do not oversell yourself though... If you do get hired and cannot live up to your bragging, you'll be out so quickly and you might even get a reputation for lying!

Question #5: What do you know about this company?

What the interviewer actually wants to know: How well-versed you are about what the company stands for, what makes the company different from the competition and what reputation it has out there.

Ideal Way to Answer: Arm yourself with basic research. With so much information out there online, it would be easy for you to get the basics down pat. You need not memorize anything but try to remember something that strikes you the most in terms of their history, goals, mission and vision, etc. If the company has been in the media lately, you may want to show where you stand with certain issues they relate to. Remember, this is not about kissing the company's ass – it's about showing that you understand what the organization is all about.

Question #6: Tell me about (a specific situation)

What the interviewer actually wants to know: How you handle different scenarios, how you respond to stress and pressure and if you can exercise the skills needed for the job.

Ideal Way to Answer: Answers will definitely vary on which scenario you are asked (and which field you are joining). Some of the situations or scenarios you may be asked include (a) how you deal with a difficult customer or client (b) working in a team with a challenging member (c) problems with your supervisor or management (d) a sample scenario that calls for initiative

Question #7: What would you do in the first three months in this post?

What the interviewer actually wants to know: How you prioritize, set goals and solve problems. They also want to know how you will be able to situate yourself in the organization.

Ideal Way to Answer: First, you put it out there that you will need time to get to know your team, the market, and all other stakeholders you will be working with. Say that you will also need to assess what has been worked on so far then you will come out with targeted goals based on the outcome that the company strives for. Make sure that your answer is realistic while still showing positive thinking and a bit of ambition. Never promise a change in system or massive sales; be reasonable so you will not be mistaken for someone who has all pipe dreams and no action.

Question #8: What do you consider most important about this position?

What the interviewer actually wants to know: Your professional or career goals and if the job you are applying for is in line with what you really want to achieve.

Ideal Way to Answer: Consider this your time to be quite candid about why you are interested in the job. Are you a people person and the job entails a lot of collaborative work? Do you like to travel and this job will let you discover new places while honing your skills? Let your interviewer know so that you can land a job that will make you happy and stay long in the company.

Interviewers want to understand your career goals and whether this job will fulfill them. After all, if you're looking for a job with lots of public contact and a highly collaborative culture, and this job is mostly solo work, it might not be the right fit for you. It's in your best interest to be candid and specific when you answer this so you land in a job that aligns with what will make you happiest.

Question #9: Where do you see yourself ___ years from now?

What the interviewer actually wants to know: What your future plans are or if you see yourself staying with them for a while. Because really – no institution likes to the vicious cycle of hiring and firing in rapid successions.

Ideal Way to Answer: Answer as truthfully yet tactfully as you can. Let the interviewer know that you have aspirations and goals to move up the ladder while still being realistic about it. It also does not hurt to let it slip what you want to learn from your exposure to their company and what you hope to contribute. Do you have big life changes planned within the time span you are asked? Let your interviewer know that you plan to get married, start a family, go back to school, move to a different country, etc.

Some may say that disclosing these matters can hurt your chances but the truth is, your prospective employer would rather know the truth. If they know and they like you anyway, they will find ways to keep you for longer.

Question #10: What is your ideal salary range?

What the interviewer actually wants to know: What compensation you expect to get if the company hires you.

Ideal Way to Answer: This question is almost always asked in job interviews, yet many job seekers are still taken aback by it. The thing is, if you are caught ill-prepared, you can end up getting a salary offer lower than the market rate and if you go overboard, you risk not getting the job. This is why, it is imperative that you find out the market rate for the job post you are applying for and use that to create the range that you will refer to. Sure, it's a bit disconcerting to talk about money but you cannot let this hinder you from getting what you deserve. Show knowledge about the market rate while matching this with your assessment of your own worth and the interviewer will be impressed.

B O N U S : Do you have any questions for me?

The cleverest of interviewers commonly end with something like "That's all the questions that I have for you right now. Do you have any questions for me?" Do you have any questions for me? – This is quite a common question yet it still stuns most interviewees.

Most people probably think, "What do you ask the person who is interviewing you?" or "Is this a trick question?" This is also why there is an apprehension to actually ask and just say "No questions, thank you." However, many interviewers will be impressed if you do ask questions to clarify your own thoughts and expectations. This is your chance to learn more about the office culture and the job position you are applying for.

However, you should never ask about anything related to benefits and pay. You should reserve these questions for when you already have an offer. So, what are the most impressive questions you can ask? Here's a quick list you can choose from (choose wisely and base it on the questions you were asked):

How has this position evolved into what it is now?

What do you enjoy most about working for this company?

What have past employees done that worked well for the job?

What is the top priority for this position over the first 90 days on the job?

What makes the managers so successful in this company?

What are the best ways for a person to collaborate more, if given the chance to work in this position?

What are some of the foreseen challenges for the person who is going to be hired in this position?

Do you have any qualms about my qualifications?

Chapter 5: Arrival To The Interview Site

Be 10 Minutes Early with Resume In-Hand
Make sure you have the right directions to the physical location of the interview. Leave home early so that you arrive at least 10 minutes before the interview. However, do not arrive more than 15 minutes early. This may not work in your favor as you may come across desperate or needy. Always bring a copy of your resume and cover letter with you when you arrive at the interview. This is expected and you will look ill prepared if you do not bring it with you.

Have a Handy List of "Goodies" Prepared
Prior to the interview, jot down some of your achievements ("goodies") in chronological order so that it can be easy memorizing them. This helps ease your nerves during an interview. This strategy has worked for each of us on many occasions. It is common to have memory issues when people get nervous at an interview. Therefore, if you have written

down the most important skills, achievements, promotions or items you want to be sure to mention that will make you stand out.

Bring Pen and Paper for Note-Taking

It is a good idea to take notes during the interview. However, you must first ask the interviewer if this is acceptable for you to do. I have never had anyone say no this question, but it is respectful to ask first and shows you have good etiquette.

Practice Interview Questions In Front of a Mirror

A good number of interview questions are based on the content of your resume, professional experience and general questions that the interviewer believes you have an answer for. Your score in these interview questions is determined by how well you prepare to have them answered. Most interviewers ask the same types of questions. Practice your answers beforehand in front of a mirror. Do research! This is vital to providing confident answers that convey that you know what you are talking about. By doing research not only on the company, but also to what is recommended as an answer, your body language and tonality will say "I believe in myself," "I know what I am talking about," and "I deserve this job because I would be good at it, as well as an asset to the company." We cannot emphasize enough the importance of doing your research about the company so you will not be caught off-guard on the day of your interview. You MUST give an answer that is confident and that shows you are properly prepared. Remember, interviewers have heard many answers before to the same questions. They can see through it if you don't properly prepare.

Some other popular ones we have received in the past are:

"Where do you see yourself in five years?"

"Why do you want to work for this company?"

"What are your biggest weaknesses?"

"What skills are you best at?"

Practice honest and natural answers to these questions in front of a mirror. This will help you remember how to answer them. Each person reading these questions will answer them differently, so go through them one-by-one and come up with your own personal answers. It is important to note that on the 'biggest weakness' question, this is sort of a trap and in my opinion, an aggressive question to ask. You need to mention a weakness that is actually a strength, but disguised as a weakness. See p.19, question 6. For example, you can say "Well, I have a habit of not looking at the clock and working long hours working on projects, especially when there is a deadline involved." By you staying and working long hours, that is really a strength, but you are using it as a weakness that you are working past the set work hours. Do not say anything here that would lower your work ethics. I suggest having a pre-planned answer for all of these, should they be asked. Feel free to use some of your own questions as well. You may want to jot down some key word answers on your notebook in case amnesia sets in during the interview.

Let's look at some of the most common interview questions you may encounter.

Answers to the most common interview questions

1) What's the most interesting thing about this job?

This question seems easy, but hiring managers are asking for a specific purpose. They want to know what your level of personal engagement is. The recruiter wants to know if you believe this job is fulfilling and challenging, as well as whether or not you will contribute to the continued growth of their business. S/he want to know what excites you about the job. Here is where you must prove yourself worthy to the recruiter. Explain what excites you about the position, how you can overcome any challenges and be sure to show your enthusiasm. Show confidence in that you know you are the proper candidate and will be a great asset to the company. You must believe you are the right fit first. Feel it in year heart, rehearse it and believe it. You have this!

2) What is your biggest achievement or a major accomplishment?

This question helps your recruiter to know what you are capable of, as well as your temperament and attitude. Make the answer relevant to the position. While most people have not done something extraordinary in the eyes of others like developing the cure for a disease, most of us can think of some large accomplishment such as leading a project that stands out above the rest. Essentially, your recruiter is trying to get you to open up and tell him or her a story about yourself as it relates to the position. Here are a few suggestions: Tell about a related, successful work project that you assisted with or led. Mention why is was successful and why it was necessary.

Another suggestion is to let him/her see your strengths by talking about a roadblock at work that you were able to triumph over and the steps you took that led you to that success.

When answering this or any other questions posed, you should do so confidently. Even if the hiring team fails to ask this question, by preparing a well constructed answer provides you with an upper hand because you can tell about what you have achieved the moment they ask a question closely related to this.

3) What's your salary expectation?

You must always prepare for this question, as there is a significant chance of encountering it at a job interview. This is one of the many questions that get candidates off-guard when being interviewed. Honestly, this subject always makes me a bit uncomfortable. However, you must have researched job salary requirements and determine your minimum salary requirement prior to going to the interview. NEVER, I repeat, never bring up the subject of salary first. Always let the recruiter make the first mention about salary.

4) Why do you think you are the best fit for this job?

You can almost expect this or a similar question when interviewing for any job. Here is where your preparedness comes in handy! Speak up your skills, similar work experience, certifications, and what type of assets you can bring to their team. Talk about your past experiences and success at work. Here is where practicing interview questions at home, as well as researching the most appropriate answers, will come into play in a large way.

5) Tell us about yourself.

Do not be tricked by this question. The interviewer is not asking about your thoughts on life or asking to hear about how your two-year-old is finally potty-trained. Answer from a professional perspective. Remember the job description for the job you are interviewing for and answer in alignment with the job requirements and skill-sets. The hiring team asks this question for a reason. You have to be precise and clear. Again, keep your special knowledge, work history, special projects, or any special accomplishment worth mentioning at the forefront when you answer. Here is where your practicing at home in front of your mirror will be vital. If you remember how you answered this question in practice at home, you can regurgitate the same information to the hiring team. Below is a simple answer to the point, which highlights the current and past skill-sets of the candidate.

"Well, currently I am a writing addict who has managed to compile a variety of articles for different companies in NYC. Before deciding to settle as a freelance writer, I used to work at a local newspaper as the editor's assistant where I was in-charge of helping to categorize and prioritize published content. I needed a more flexible schedule at the time, which is why I took on a freelance role. I am now seeking this position in a full-time capacity where I can stabilize my career while contributing to growth of the organization."

Don't go off on a tangent unless the recruiter further questions you on a component of your answer. Then go ahead and answer him or her, but be sure to get back on-track in line with the question the recruiter asked you originally. You can circle back by saying something like, "...so getting back to what you wanted to know about my past position as a credit analyst..." Remember, you are not only being judged by the answers you provide, but on the quality of your speaking skills, remembering to stay on-topic and the quality of your words, tonality, attitude, posture, among other elements. You are a whole package being judged strongly against likely many other candidates. The competition is tough and so you must be as well.

6) What would you say your biggest weakness is?

Answer this in a way that disguises a strength as a weakness. Some hiring managers ask you questions deliberately to find out whether you are the best candidate for the job and to try to sneak information out of you. The trick here is not to give a weakness at all. Find a quality about you that is a strength, but give it a weak twist. For example, "I tend to work be a work-a-holic and lose track of time at work, especially when working on large projects." You are revealing the fact that you are a very hard-working individual, while in reality, in the eyes of the recruiter, that is a strength, not a weakness.

Do not say "I can't, I won't, I don't understand, it's impossible for me to..." or any variation of these. This is a death sentence. Instead, be honest and humble, but do not reveal a quality about yourself that is an obvious weakness. This will limit your chances of getting the job. The recruiter is simply trying to scan you to see if you can be weeded out early. If you can show that you are an honest and direct person with flaws not unlike any other human, it will most likely keep them interested in you.

Speaking Up To Get Hired

Since first impressions are always the most important, the way you come across to the interviewer has a lasting impression. This means that you have to make it count.

Speak clearly and have a friendly attitude. Smile! Smile! Smile!

Idle chat is acceptable at the beginning or end of the interview if you sense that the interviewer is open to it. You can tell by the topics s/he mentions and the language used in the way the conversation is lead. If s/he goes off topic about something personal, for example, a picture of her dog on her desk, it is ok to follow the lead. This is a good opportunity to build some rapport. (See below for rapport building tips).

Chapter 6: Acing the Job Interview

So, you have got your resume done, you have scheduled your interview, and you already know what to wear... what's next?

The next thing is to be ready for the most important thing – the interview day.

You know that job interviews can be nerve-racking, that's why you're here; particularly because the nature of a job interview can be surprising. Normally, an employer adds an entirely new series of question to help them determine not just the applicant's skill set, knowledge, and dreams, but also a better understanding of their personality. This chapter will explain to you, important tips about you must know to succeed in your interview and get more chances to get the job you are dreaming of.

Effective Speaking Techniques

You might have a very impressive resume and you have extremely refined attire for your interview suit, but you have to know that it's not only about the paper and the looks. Most of the time, the way you sound when you speak is more important. However, a lot of job hunters let careless speech habits drop their probabilities of having that desirable job.

Below are the most common language mistakes applicants commit during the job interview and the effective ways how to stop them from sabotaging your chance:

Unnecessary Fillers

Filler words like "ah," "um," "you know," or "like" tell the interviewer you are not ready and give them the impression that you have never experienced being in such situation before. A good strategy to follow is to think before saying anything, have some pauses, and take a few breaths once you lose your drift. It's normal for people to utter an occasional "uh," but try not to say it at every beginning of the sentence.

Up-talk

A singsong or rising tone at the end of every sentence makes a hesitant impression and makes it seem like you are asking a question rather than making a conclusive statement. You have to sound confident when you are selling yourself during the interview. Take your pitch down whenever you end a sentence in order to avoid speaking up.

Grammatical Errors

The job interviewer might question your education when using improper slang or grammar. Expressions like "ain't," "nah," "me and my friend" and others are not appropriate. Make sure you're speaking in whole sentences and that tenses are correct. We always hear advice telling us we should relax, and while it's true, you shouldn't be too relaxed that you end up sounds like you're just talking to a longtime friend.

Untidy Speech

Smearing words together or omitting their endings harms the lucidity of the message you want to send. In order to avoid slurring and boost understanding, try to speak at a slow phase. List down your most commonly misstated words and practice saying them in a recorder, and try to improve. So, when the interview day comes, you will never make the same mistake again.

Speed Talking

While it's normal for everyone to be slightly nervous during a job interview, the last thing you want to happen is to make the important information to fly all over the place. A fast speaking rate is not easy to follow, and the impression to fast talkers is nervous and tense. Decelerate your speeding heart by following some sort of breathing exercises before the big day. In order to avoid rushing, focus on the question, and before answering, count two beats beforehand. Once you finish a sentence, count again before carrying on. Don't be afraid of quick, sudden silence. Again, pausing is very important part of good communication technique. Anyway, the interviewer requires a few seconds to understand what you just said.

Practice these methods on a daily basis until the unnecessary wordings you do are no longer a part of your speech pattern. Keep in mind you don't want to use the filler and expression words as if you are talking to a friend. Again, your goal here is to sound professional.

Body Language

Paying attention to the way your body moves is as important as practicing you speech pattern before going on a job interview. Your body language offers an instant and vast perception into your state of mind. Most veteran employers can sense nervousness, indecision, haughtiness, confidence, and a lot of other feelings expressed by the applicants while they are interviewing them.

Body language changes from person to person, yet it still offers the same signals to an interviewer when appraising your responses throughout the interview process. Learn how you can use affirmative body language while in an interview. Your goal is to make the interviewer think that you are confident through your body language, which sequentially will improve your responses and increase your chances to get the job. Below are some body languages you must focus on during your interview.

Handshake: Shaking hands the interviewer will give them a good impression. This simple gesture will help you make an approachable and professional image. Don't forget that the handshake should be firm and have the same pressure. Imitate the grip of the interviewer; it evades any dominant feelings.

Sitting down: When sitting down, do it slowly and don't get too comfortable right away. If you appear to be too relaxed, it may give the employer an impression that you are arrogant. Don't flip the chair around, sway from side to side or loafing back in the chair.

Posture:

If there is something you have to be relaxed, that is your posture. Sit straight or lean forward a bit to showcase a confident appearance. You must not fiddle. Keep your feet close by together or crossed and your body fronting the interviewer.

Eye Contact:

Look the interviewer in the eyes when responding to questions. However, don't keep eye contact with the interviewer the whole time; you don't want to come up as creepy. The goal here is to look honest and straightforward and blinking is important.

Facial Expressions:

Smiling always lowers the level of nervousness, so keep smiling; this will display your eagerness. But then again, don't look TOO eager or blank that you do not seem to care.

Humor:

If you can, show appropriate humor while getting interviewed to relax your anxieties and lightens up the vibe in the situation. Again, an APPROPRIATE humor only! The proper amount of humor will show that you're a confident person who's relaxed and can control rough situations.

Hand movements:

Using your hands while expressing while talking will show positive effects on your responses. Make use of your hands to describe your answers or explain your ideas. As much as possible, keep your hands visible throughout the process.

Keep Interest:

Show your employer that you are interested and paying attention by nodding your head in approval and showing that understand every word he says. Avoid crossing your arms, finger drumming, thumb twiddling, and other fidgeting behaviors.

Pay attention to your body language and think of it as a free and natural as your style of speaking, and don't be too meticulous or rehearsed. When your movements are in tune with your answers, you will seem assertive and on top of things.

Common Questions You Can Prepare For

Of course, there are questions that are unexpected and will require you to improvise to give the best answer you can. However, there are still some questions that are frequently asked during a job interview and it is always a good idea to be prepared for them.

So, in this chapter we give you the 3 commonly asked questions in a job interview you must be prepared of. Obviously, we cannot guarantee that these questions will be asked, but getting ready if they asked would help you a lot.

"How would you describe yourself?"

In many cases, this question is used as an opening question. Clearly, it intends to know if your personality suits the native of the job you are applying for. So, your answer should be focused on that path.

But there's one thing you have to keep in mind. Depending on who is asking the question, your answer may differ. For instance, if the company's CEO is the one to ask you this, they'd probably expect you to be independent and creative, a person who accepts challenges and can easily get away from it. On the other hand, if an HR manager asks you the same question your response must highlight your teamwork qualities, and how you would be suitable for the working environment of the company.

Focus on the good qualities that you can apply to your working environment rather than your personal life.

"Why did you think you are suitable for this job? Why should we hire you?"

This is the question that could make or break you. If you can come up with the exact answer the interviewer wants to hear, then you'll probably get the job, otherwise, you'll end up finding another company to send your resume in. It's also a question asked by most interviewers as for them, it is a great way to determine whether they should hire you or not.

Your answer must reflect the fact that you're entirely well-matched with that specific company. The answer to this particular question must show that you did research about the company and the particular job you are applying for. You should be familiar with their activity, their clients, their goals, achievements, and other aspects that represent the company's background and operation. And derived from your research, you should prove that you're a possibly valuable benefit for the company.

"Did you leave your previous job or were you laid off? Why?"

Clearly, the purpose of these questions is to determine if you'll be a pain for the company eventually. Furthermore, the interviewers would be interested to know how long you're willing to stay in their company. Most companies are seeking long-term employees, as training and hiring can be extra expenses for the company.

So, don't say that you were laid off because of differences you had with your former employer, in case you were actually laid off. In the event you were fired because of an error, say that you have learned from your previous mistakes. And if ever you left your job since you had to move or because of other personal reason, make sure that you let the interviewer know, and you can work for them on a long-term basis.

To end this post, here are some tips that you may find helpful:

-Your response shouldn't sound rehearsed
-Take some time before answering any question in case you need time to know
-Keep the answers short and sweet
-Make sure the answers you give sound reliable

-Last, of all, try to put yourself in the interviewer's situation and imagine the answers you'd want to hear from someone when you asked them the same thing.

General Tips You Must Know

1. Sell it, don't tell it

In a job interview, your goal is to "sell" yourself. Let me give you an example: The interviewer may ask you how many individuals you managed in your previous job. These are the possible answers and one of them is better...

Telling: "50 people."

Selling: "I managed 50 people on my previous job. This number includes both support and professional personnel. In addition to managing them, I also managed all hiring and recruitment and activities. Furthermore, my team boosted sales by over 40% in my first year in the company reducing the company's overall costs by 10%".

Be precise, but don't go overboard.

2. Turn Negative into Positive

Let's say you are asked about your experience in managing people but you've never done that in the past. The response that you will think is right is, to tell the truth, and say "No, I don't have experience on that field." While this is acceptable, you can turn this response better.

Instead, you can use the related experience to response the question and highlight your skills. A better alternative answer would be, "I didn't have experience in managing people, as I focused on the line where I am more passionate it which is (insert your line of work here.)" This is an honest and at the same time constructive.

3. Use the Big to highlight the Small

Let's say the interviewer asks you if you have any experience with accounting. In order to establish your thoughts, make your answer flow flawlessly, and make it simple for the interviewer to comprehend your precise experience in that field. Begin with the "big" with an impression of your experience in accounting transactions; just some sentences to explain your general range and depth of experience. Then, follow it up with some specific, "small" accomplishments, ventures, or highlights that are straightly related. You may state your involvement in setting salary, expenses reports, and anything related. Basically, you are telling the things you know about and how well you did on it before.

4. Remember that you have passed the initial interview

Before getting to the job interview, keep in mind that you've passed your initial test – You've been invited or granted a job interview derived from your impressive resume, good reputation, and performance derived from a telephone initial interview. If you're going to get interviewed by top administrators of the company, it is an indication that they really are interested in you. Their time is very important. They would not be meeting with you if they were not interested. Treat the interview knowing you have got them hooked. We wouldn't suggest you be cocky, though. instead, use this knowledge to relax and show them your best shot. Be confident, calm, and apply the objective that you're there to sign a contract and end their hunt for an employee for the specific position.

5. Take action

It's possible that something in your resume, experiences, or skills might have been ignored. Maybe, it was your previous experience with Logistics or Accounting. It's your accountability to present this data in the discussion before the interview ends.

You can say something like, "Before we finish the interview, I would want to tell you some more things about myself that are related to the position I am applying to your company." Then proceed with the details, and makes sure that it's relevant to the job you are trying to apply for.

Reasonably, the process of the job interview is stressful and is not an easy situation. Remember that your professional life is at serious risk. Keep in mind that it's important to walk into every interview with a plan of actually getting your wanted result, and work to achieve that goal. Prove and exemplify your experience and qualifications. Silently take control of the process of the interview and imagine something that will take you to the position you are trying to aim.

With that being said, there are people who sound great on paper, but when the moment they start answering, they fail miserably. Here are more tips to remember when you're on an interview.

Talking too much

Please, don't talk too much. Yes, you have to take part in the discussion with the interviewer, but allow them to take control of the pace. Speak deliberately, clearly, and slowly. Keep eye contact, but do not stare.

Past Employers

Don't say anything bad about your past employers. No matter how mean your last boss was, saying bad things about your boss would not describe them, but instead, describe you. It's going to be your loss. When you find it hard to describe your past employer, keep in mind that you have to keep positive and think about the good things about them. Of course, there were some good traits you known in your former employers, try to focus on them.

Don't be late

Traffic, failed alarm, losing direction, or anything excuse shouldn't be a reason. Never be late for your job interview. At the same time, however, don't show up too early, this will make them feel like you're rushing them, especially if there are no other waiting. Being factual is one of the best trains of an employee, and the interviewer is going to appreciate it if you get there on time.

Be nice to the receptionist

The receptionist normally is the first part of the company you're going to meet, and so, it's important that you give them the best impression. Be respectful and not be too talkative. The receptionist holds the control to bring you to the interviewer in a good or bad light. Never underestimate the authority a receptionist can offer.

Pay, Benefits, and Vacation Leave

Again, don't get too comfortable, and one of the signs of you being too comfortable is asking about inappropriate questions. This includes questions about the pay, benefits, or vacation leave during the first interview. Keep in mind that a job interview is supposed to determine if you're the right candidate for the job. Your goal is to get an offer of employment.

If you get the job, you'll definitely have another meeting, this is where you can start discussing the pay, benefits, and the leaves toy can have. During this time, you're certain that your skills and knowledge are important to the employer, and you will have the right to know everything about your profits.

Chapter 7: Learning From Mistakes And Being Fearless

Every single day, you expose yourself to failure and risks as you go up the corporate ladder. Every experience has its valuable lessons. If you learn from your mistakes, you are actually developing a leadership trait. By observing how executives deal with failure, you can actually learn a lot from their mistakes. You can quickly recognize a mistake and efficiently make decisions to either correct it instantly or seek to learn from it. In general, you can generate immediate feedback if you're open to recognize your mistake and learn.

Allow Yourself To Make Mistakes

You have to learn to accept challenges or assignments which will most probably fail. You have to get out of your comfort zone which may expose you to some risks because it will let you grow and develop important leadership skills. If you continuously search for situations where in you can play it safe, your ability to recover and learn will be reduced. On the other hand, you have to exercise great care when you take on risks. You only have to allow sufficient risks so that you'll grow and not encounter catastrophic failures. Lastly, you have to ensure that you get up on your feet immediately so that other people will know that you've learned your lessons.

Accept Your Mistakes

If you made a mistake, you can turn it to an opportunity. However, you must first accept accountability for it. If your ideas or projects don't do well as planned, you can't blame other people or some other outside forces for your failure. Although it's difficult to accept accountability, you have to show that you're willing to accept new things because these will emphasize the lessons you learned and will make you take steps so that the mistake won't happen again.

Turning Mistakes To Opportunities

What you do right now may not make you eligible for future success or promotion. It can actually be a hindrance. If you're doing well in your present job, you may become overconfident. Your being a current standout may actually be a negative factor for future performance. You have to show that you can easily overcome any difficulty and adapt well to new positions.

A senior executive will be promoted based on his learning agility and not on their past performances. His ability to respond to change and self-awareness are the two most important traits that he possesses. If you want to go up the corporate ladder, you have to embrace responsibilities, make errors, and learn from them.

What You Can Learn From Your Mistakes

After graduating from college and taking on your first job, you surely have made a lot of mistakes which taught you a lot of things about yourself and your path to success. These errors are essential to your professional development. Everyone has his faire share of mistakes while going up the ladder of success. However, there are important lessons which you have to learn as you go along your professional journey.

By learning from your mistakes, you'll learn how to manage change. If you don't adapt to changes, you won't be able to control your mistakes. You have to be prepared to adapt to these changes. It is important that you remain focused on what's to come. You can't avoid making mistakes if you don't look ahead and consider what may happen in the future. You have to be able to perceive and prepare for changes which may come. You have to have the right attitude to continue moving forward.

Furthermore, you have to be open to new possibilities. If you're prepared for anything, you will be able to welcome any change easily. You see things with a fresh mindset and by being open minded, you will uncover every possible opportunity from your mistakes. You'll be challenged to improve yourself by learning new skills. However, if you resist changes, you'll just regret what you've done.

Lastly, it is important that, aside from skill and focus, you also learn to look at the big picture. You have to have the right perspective and visualize how your present situation contributes to your overall career plan. If you focus only on day-to-day activities, you tend to make short-term gains only. You must be able to set your goals for a career you really want and can be proud of.

How To Overcome Fear Of Failure

The meaning of failure differs from person to person because each of us has our own belief systems, values, and benchmarks. It may be a failure to an individual but for another person, it may be a great learning experience. There are people who fear failure and they fail to achieve their goals because of it.

A person may fear failure because he has unsupportive or critical parents. He may have been humiliated or undermined when he was a child and the experience caused negative feelings when he became an adult. He may have experienced a traumatic situation, which caused him to fear failure.

If you're someone who fears failure, you may have experienced the following symptoms: self-sabotage, low self-esteem, and perfectionism. People who live very cautiously are those who don't go anywhere. They stay put. It's as if they're not really living. If you don't want to be like these people, you have to look at failure not as the end but as an incredible experience which you can learn from. If you fail at something, you have to search for the lessons, which will allow you to grow and refrain from making the same mistake again.

You may suffer from bad decisions in your life. Some doors may be closed. You may fail and stumble. However, you have to think of all those people who failed in the past but are successful now. You have to search for opportunities from each of your failures.

Fear of failure can be lessened through analysis of all possible results. It is but normal to fear the unknown. However, you can reduce this fear if you study every possible outcome which may result from your decision. Positive thinking is also a powerful method of neutralizing self-sabotage and building self-confidence. In addition, you have to prepare for the worst-case scenario. It may be rational to fear for the worst possible outcome but if you recognize it, you can seek for help.

If you don't like to fail, you have to develop a contingency plan in case something goes wrong with your decision. This way, you'll feel more confident about moving along. If you fear failure, you may not be comfortable about goal setting. However, these goals must be made if you want to succeed in life. You can try visualization when you set your goals. For example, you can imagine your life after you've become successful. This will motivate you to try your best to reach your goals.

In some cases, visualization may have a negative effect because you may feel some form of negativity after visualizing your success. You can prevent this from happening if you set some small goals instead. These goals must be challenging but not very overwhelming so that your confidence will get a big boost after accomplishing them.

How To Overcome Fear Of Searching For Work

It is normal to have fears when you look for a job. You may fear that no employer will hire you. However, if you carefully check each job advertisement, you'll be comforted that you have a chance of being hired if you make an effort. On the other hand, if you've already made a great effort but you're still not being hired, it may be time to look for a lower-level job.

However, it is good if you set your sights on a higher career goal now. Your self-esteem may be affected temporarily but you can actually redirect your search to more appropriate positions and succeed in it. If you just take a step backward, you'll be able to give yourself time to grow, be calmer, and then go up the corporate ladder once again. The important thing to remember is that there are various ways to succeed.

You may find it embarrassing to let your colleagues and friends know that you're searching for work. In fact, you may even feel afraid that they'll find out, especially if these people are well-employed. You may think that they will look down on you and believe that you're a loser. However, your colleagues and friends are your best source for job leads.

To reduce this feeling of fear, you need not announce to the whole world that you're desperate because you can't find a job. You can just honestly say that you've been laid off and you're trying to search for better work opportunities. You can tell your friends what position you're looking for and ask for referrals.

If it's your first time to search for a job, you may the feeling that your life will be less fun because you'll soon have to give up a lot of the fun things you did when you start working. Although you'll feel temporarily sad about it, you'll find work more enjoyable because you'll be able to contribute not only to your family but to the society as well. If you're doing ethical work, even the smallest job can be contributory. You'll find it uplifting if you work. In fact, other people will respect you if you tell them you're finally working.

If you've been unhappy in your previous job, you may have fears about finding another work. You may think that you'll be unsuccessful or unhappy in your next job. You can lessen this fear by thinking that you can also vet your employer during job interviews. This way, you can decide not to take the offer if you feel an unhappy vibe about the company.

In addition, if you search for better work opportunities, you may feel sad about your loved ones who don't have the same opportunities as you do. You may feel that they'll compare you with themselves and they'll feel inferior. However, you have to remind yourself that you're paying a steep price if you deny yourself a better job. You can actually encourage your loved ones to find better jobs, too. In addition, you can explain to them that having a good job isn't the only factor in determining the worth of a person.

Lastly, you may think that you're selling yourself when you look for a job. You may believe you're being pushy in promoting yourself. Although there are opportunities that may come to you easily, most jobs are difficult to come by. You need not oversell yourself though. If you oversell yourself, your employer may think that you can do a lot of things. Thus, it is best to reveal who you really are when you go a job interview. Your honesty is important to your success.

Some Interview Questions And Answers

Question: What is your greatest fear? Why this may be asked: The interviewer wants to know what you want from the potential job. For example, if you say you fear of being stuck in a job with no room for growth, he'll know that your first priority is career development. In addition, he may want to test how well you prepared for the interview or how quickly you respond to a question.

Possible answer: I don't have any fears about this job because I am experienced. I'm not afraid to do things even if I've not done them before. I'll take on a challenging task anytime. However, my biggest fear is that because of my tendency to accept various duties and responsibilities, these may set me off track from my career goals.

In answering the question, you should avoid answers which aren't related to the work you're applying for. Although you may include some humor in your reply, you are really not answering the question correctly. You have to give answers which are related to your career goals, your skills, and your work.

You can relate a fear with being unfulfilled in your career. A lot of interviewers want to opt for candidates who are very passionate about their success. This question aims to give you a chance to explain to the interviewer about your personal drives for success in your career.

Chapter 8: Common Interview Questions

How did you learn about this job?

Why do you want this job?

What are your biggest strengths?

What are your biggest weaknesses

Tell me more about yourself?

What are you the best fit for this position?

What are your salary expectations?

Why did you leave your last job?

What are you future goals?

Tell me about an experience where you had to deal with a difficult situation.

How do you handle failure?

How do you handle success?

What makes you stand out from the rest of the applicants?

Where do you see yourself in 5 years? 10 years?

What do you look to accomplish in the first 30 days? 90 days?

Why are you interested in this company specifically?

What is your greatest motivation in life?

How do you handle stressful situations?

Tell me about a time when you disagreed with your boss or manager.

What do you like the least and the most about this industry?

What are your favorite hobbies and pastimes?

Are you more of a leader or a follower? Why?

Why was there a gap in your employment between [date] and [date]?

What can you uniquely bring to this company that others can't?

If money wasn't an option, what would you do with your life?

How do you handle mistakes? Tell me about a time when you did.

What is your single-most greatest accomplishment?

How would go about firing somebody?

What is your ideal work environment?

What is your leadership style?

What is the toughest decision you've had to make in the past 9 months?

What was your salary in your previous job?

What are your top three traits?

What traits would you look for when hiring somebody?

What are our company values?

What is our company's highest priority?

What other companies are you considering?

Have you been fired before? If so, why?

How would your previous boss and coworkers describe you?

If you could be any animal, what would it be?

What is your favorite website?

What is your favorite book?

What is your favorite magazine/journal?

What makes you the most uncomfortable?

Are you willing to travel/relocate?

Would you be willing to work 40+ hours a week?

Would you be willing to work on holidays?

What makes you wake up every morning?

Do you know the name of our CEO?

If you started your own organization, what would your top 5 values be?

Are you good or bad at asking for assistance?

What was your college experience like?

What were your responsibilities in your last job?

How do you deal with unresponsive coworkers or clients?

unsure of how to move forward. How did you respond?

You find yourself working on a project that you cannot complete because your colleague has not submitted their work. How do you respond?

Do you prefer written or verbal communication?

What do you do if there is a breakdown of communication on your team?

What would you do if you saw an employee stealing supplies?

What would you do if somebody took credit for your ideas?

How well do you think this interview is going so far?

Are there any questions that I haven't asked you yet?

Do you have any questions for me?

Chapter 9: Developing the Q&A

Overview

Once you have identified the factors that help or hinder your ability to accomplish your objective, the next step is to develop the questions you intend to ask your interviewee. The first thing you need to know about developing your questions is that no question will be random or without a specific purpose. Other than follow-up or spontaneous questions, every question you ask should be a **strategic** question intended to elicit the kind of answer that moves you closer to your goal. Some questions are intended to establish a rapport, while others are intended to get the interviewee thinking about your qualifications and who you are as a person. Unplanned questions are the ones that will emerge as the dialogue evolves (e.g. follow-up or spur-of-the-moment questions).

Developing the Right Questions

The type of questions you ask will depend largely on your goals and level of experience in your career field. However, to truly understand what questions to pose, you must first understand the nature of this type of interview. While the informational interview serves many purposes, the ones we are primarily concerned with achieving are **differentiation** and **creating exposure.** The former is what separates you from the other hopefuls, while the latter helps expand your professional network. Both increase your chances of getting hired. When it comes to establishing rapport, a basic rule of thumb (meaning my rule) is to ask questions that get the interviewee talking about him or herself. When you can get people to share anecdotal stories about themselves it creates a bond of sorts. People appreciate you caring enough to learn about"their story". The more you can connect personally with the interviewee, the more likely they are to become invested in helping you achieve your goals.

When developing your questions, think about your particular situation and the type of information you would need to know to help you to achieve that objective. For example, if you are a recent college graduate or soon-to-be graduate, you might ask the interviewee questions about how they got their start in their field, some of the challenges they experienced, personal lessons they learned along the way, or things they might have done differently. These types of questions elicit not only very useful information, but also inspire the interviewee toward personal reflection. The more an interviewee is willing to share of him or herself, the greater the likelihood of establishing the kind of rapport that leads to relationships. For your reference, I provide a comprehensive list of sample questions at the end of the book designed to inspire questions specific to your situation. **Click here for the list.**

One thing to keep in mind is that the Q&A is not a one-size-fits-all activity. Each interviewee is different and the questions must be tailored as such. For example, in your research you may have uncovered that the interviewee faced a specific challenge or accomplished something extraordinary, to which you may want to ask a question that addresses that fact. Feel free to ask about those things. It is also okay to ask questions about their personal motivations or professional triumphs and setbacks, past and present. However, let discretion and good judgement be your guide. Do not ask questions that delve too deeply into their personal lives.

Feel free to ask the interviewee about the strategies he or she has previously employed or **intends** to employ to advance their own career. Above all, be creative, and make your questions count.

You have a limited time to conduct the interview, so think of about 15-20 questions and then cull it down to your top 10 or so. Keep the other questions in your back pocket in case you have time left. However, chances are good that you will expend all of your time on your primary questions. It is also quite conceivable that the two of you really hit it off and simply get caught up in the conversation.

This brings me to my final point on this topic. Do not focus on making the interview a mechanical Q&A session. The goal is to be conversational. Yes, you are there to ask questions and gain their insights, but be mindful of communication cues that facilitate and promote meaningful dialogue. Try to have fun as you get to know your interviewees, but above all, make sure they get to know _you._ The more you can create a relaxed, conversational environment, the more likely you are to establish a rapport and engender a sense of goodwill and trust with the interviewee. Keep in mind that you are the one in control of the Q&A. As you go, so too will the interview. What I mean is that if you have a positive attitude, chances are good the interviewee will as well. If you appear less than enthused in your Q&A, chances are that the interviewee will be less than forthcoming with helpful information. A good attitude will be your best friend throughout the entire informational interview process.

Chapter 10: The Things To Do & Avoid

Before An Interview

The night before your job interview make sure to stay in and get yourself prepared for your interview, reviewing perhaps the question that you will ask your future boss. If your friends call and want you to go out drinking and socializing, politely refuse and tell them you are staying in. Do not succumb to peer pressure because this could end up costing you the job you are interviewing for. You do not want to show up at your interview looking tired and hungover and smelling bad for your interview.

Don't Schedule Anything the Day Before Interview

You should try and take the day off before your interview or try not to schedule anything for that day. Instead spend that day getting yourself prepared for the interview on the following day. Make sure that your outfit that you are planning on wearing is not all full of wrinkles but is nice and pressed. Give it a nice around over the night before hanging it up nicely. Have the shoes that you are wearing for the interview nice and polished sitting under your suit. Make sure that you have set your alarm clock so that you can get up in plenty of time to shower before your interview and get yourself nice and well groomed.

Having a list of the things that you want to do in preparation for your interview is a good idea. Spend the morning going over your list and checking off what you have taken care of to be prepared. Always show up early in an interview as it proves that you are taking the interview seriously and very keen in the position.

Use Google Map

You want to make sure that you will arrive for your interview at least half an hour early. You must take into consideration traffic jams. If you are not sure of the exact location of your interview, it is a good idea to do a dry run there perhaps on the day before the interview. Have a look on Google map to get the directions of the location. It is best to do a dry run then you can time how long it takes you to get from where you live to the location. You do not want to show up late in an interview as this is more than likely to cost you your chance of getting the job. Showing up late to an interview is basically giving the future boss the message that you are not a dependable person.

Wash Your Hands Just Before the Interview

While you are sitting waiting to be called for your interview ask the secretary where the washroom is, then go there and wash your hands to prevent them from becoming sticky and sweaty. You do not want to offer your future boss a wet sticky hand, this will not be off to a good start, they will see this as you not being a confident individual. So, make sure that you wash and dry your ends very thoroughly. Check your appearance and make sure all is looking good. Make any final adjustments to your hair and makeup.

Dress up for Interview without Being Noticed by Your Current Boss

Many companies today allow their employees to dress business casual, or even allow them to wear jeans. You don't want to dress up in the morning making your current boss suspicious of what you may be up to. You might be better to take half the day or a full day off on the day of your interview. You could also drive somewhere perhaps home if you live close enough and change into the suit for your interview.

I think the best choice if possible is to take a day off so that you can get ready at home making sure you are dressed properly. You don't want to be dressing somewhere else and end up parts of your clothing are stuck in others, in the rush to get ready you missed this. Walking into an interview with your outfit out of whack could end up costing you that job. When you are getting ready in the comfort of your own home you can take the time to give yourself a good look over and make sure you look the part.

Chapter 11: Interview: The Final Frontier

You have prepared your resume, sent it, gotten accepted for an interview. You are done networking, asking for help and accepting any that came your way. Now comes the real test- the Interview.

The purpose of conducting an interview is to gain practical knowledge regarding your capabilities and to ascertain whether whatever you claimed in your resume is actually true or not. You need to handle this stage very cautiously otherwise all that you worked for till now will be futile. Below are given some of the handy tips to be kept in mind while preparing for an interview and appearing for one:

Whoever said looks don't matter hasn't given an interview

Your physical appearance is as important as your intellectual capability. It is not sufficient to have crammed up a lot of facts about the place you are applying at. You must appear smart, suave and properly dressed. Some tips that can help you in this regard:

- Choose a suit that goes with your personality. Do not go for a brightly colored one. Choose a somber one, preferably grey or off white.

- Trim your beard or shave completely. A shaggy looking face is generally despised and doesn't let you score brownie points.

- Take care of your face before heading out for an interview. Apply creams according to the weather. You don't have to be the hunk of the room; just don't appear casual is all.

- Pay attention to your shoes. A pointed shoe should be avoided since it doesn't go well with everyone's personality. It always safe to choose simple yet elegant footwear. Coloring shouldn't be mismatching with your suit.

- Your tie should compliment your suit or your shirt, if you have decided to go in simple formals.

- Cut your nails or clean them before appearing. It is tiny things like these that go against you in the overall report card. You may not realize it but the interviewers pay attention to each and every detail of your personality. It is therefore, advisable to look after it as best as possible, especially so a few days preceding the interview.

Posture of your body

The way you stand, sit, walk and place your legs determine to a large extent how the interviewers see you. Make sure you do not come across as a sluggard because of the way you walk. Sit straight as that conveys a good impression to those sitting across the table.

Body language

Do not ignore the psychological implications you leave behind by your body language. Learn to use body language to your advantage. Neglecting body language will only lead to misleading and often gross assumptions being formed about you.

Sitting in a cross armed position is a sign of hostility. In any circle, when you sit cross armed, it implies that you are not welcome to any opinion other than your own. Similarly, shaky legs imply nervousness. Nervousness is one quality no interviewer appreciates. It shows lack of self-confidence- another undesirable trait in a prospective employee.

Talking style

Make sure you are good at your language fluency and command. Safely assuming most interviews use English as the communication means, it is advisable to learn speaking brief yet informative sentences. Some more tips can be found below-

● Do not be flashy regarding your vocabulary. You may know a lot of pish posh words but that amount of vocabulary-expression may put some people off. Some interviewers prefer simplicity over show off oriented speaking skills.

● Do not beat around the bush while trying to answer a question. Those sitting across the table are intelligent and wise people. They can tell if you try to bluff. Attempting so will only count against you.

• If you do not know answer to a particular question, politely say so. Do not attempt to venture into the territory of guesses and half-answers. It is not necessary that you answer every question that's asked to you. But when you admit lack of knowledge it shows that you brave enough to admit your flaws.

• Keep your tone medium. Do not sound timid or too loud. Either tone has a negative impact on your personality. Vary your tone only when required. Use formal yet understandable words. Remember, you are not talking to a set of friends; you are talking to please people into hiring you.

Brush up well beforehand

It is supremely vital that you do your homework well. There are three areas you must be up to date with. One is the area and nature of work. The very fact that you are applying for a job in the mentioned office implies that you have knowledge of the nature of work that's done there.

If you gain mastery over the same, you are going to sail through your interview. Don't forget to brush up on everything you have claimed in your resume. They might just ask something like "so you have mentioned debate competitions. What topic did you debate on?". If you fumble or do not give a satisfactory answer, chances are there will be suspicions cast over your claims.

The second thing you need to research well before walking into the interview room is the history, working and achievements of the particular office. Interviewers are largely impressed when job seekers display an in depth knowledge about their workplace's origins and current position in the market.

The third and final thing you need to do your homework on is everything you have studied till your graduation. If you had opted for doing an honors degree, it holds more significance over other subjects.

Appear positive

It is important that your appearance isn't dull and disinterested. Don a look that's positive and optimistic. Self-confidence should ooze out of every pore of your body. Guard against over confidence and try to be as humble as possible. Despite how the interview goes, thank them in the end for a mere opportunity.

Keep a track of results

Some companies have a policy of simply publishing their interview results on their official websites on the internet. Keep visiting these sites for regular updates about result publications. Make sure you gave them the correct contact details in case a need for individual and personal contacting arose.

Put in more than one bait

Job hunting is like fishing. You may not trap a single fish in one lake; the trick is to try another lake! Do not pin all your hopes on one company. It pays well to have applied for interviews in more than one office. You never know which one opens its doors for you.

Job hunting is a very vital process of a person's life. It establishes him in a life of work and comfort. The most important part of the entire process is the interview stage. This stage plays a pivotal role in determining whether you land a job or not. Pay attention to all the points mentioned in this chapter and you will stand a good chance. Do not neglect this stage's relevance as it is that point in the grand plot of job searching that ultimately has a say in your life.

Miscellaneous tips:

Here are some handy tips in order to fare well in a job interview:

• Make it a point to arrive at least half an hour early. This gives you ample time to settle in and get acquainted with the new surroundings.

• Check your nose hair before walking into the room. It is a huge turn off for those interviewing to constantly notice thin strands of black creeping out of your nose.

• Use the restroom well in advance. Make sure your tie, make-up, formal wear are all in order and there's nothing revolting about your appearance. Remember to appear decent yet classy.

• Ask questions. If you do not know the right answer to a question, ask back. Do not hesitate to ask the interviewer the right answer as this will show that you are eager to learn. You can also ask about the work environment and all the details regarding the nature of your work.

• Do not lie or exaggerate. A lie or an exaggerated truth shows you the door right away. When you lie, you break their trust even before you have got the chance to gain it!

• Talk about your failures. Interviewers are impressed more with your failure stories than your achievements. Mention your phobias and really embarrassing failures and how you overcame them. This will send across a positive message about your mentality.

• Firm handshakes show that you are a confident applicant. Do not let these handshakes last longer than three seconds. Make sure your palms are not sweaty before shaking hands.

• A smile never hurts. Smiles have the power to convey extreme positivity and heightened optimism. No one ever gets offended by a simple smile. Wear one.

- Notice the body language of the interviewer. Lean forward if you have to; it shows that you are more interested to learn. Use your hands to express yourself at times. It shows them that you rely upon more than your tongue to relay your talent.

- Look straight into the eye of the interviewer. Besides spelling confidence, it signifies that you are not nervous about being asked questions. Make sure you don't end up staring at the interviewer.

- Do not broach sensitive issues while talking. You may be asked to talk about any random topic under the sun but exercise common sense while talking about things like politics, racism and sexism. One wrong word and the dominoes start falling!

- Do not touch the topic of salary on your own. If asked, you can always say that is up to them. Mention that you expect to be paid according to what you deserve.

Chapter 12: Top 10 Personal Interview Questions

What will you say if your work gets criticized?

Tips: You should be able to accept criticism with an open mind as anything said against your work is to help you improve. Even if you do not like people criticizing, do not let it out. If you look at it positively, it gives you an opportunity to groom yourself as a professional.

Answer: I take criticism positively as it allows me improve myself on both professional and personal ends.

Can you tell me any three of your pet peeves?

Tips: The best way is to not let out your weaknesses yourself. Do not share your pet peeves even if you have any. Just work around a nice answer to handle this question. A sample answer is given below.

Answer: I do not have any particular pet peeves. When something bothers me, I analyze the situation and then take appropriate measures to set things straight.

What are your biggest Strengths?

Tips: This is the best time to present you as the most worthy candidate for the job. Assess what are the most wanted skills for the job and match them against your natural strengths. You can be an excellent motivating leader or a person with extra ordinary logical skills to overcome conflict situations.

Answer: My biggest strength would be my superb command on blah blah.

Tell me about your closest friend.

Tips: There is no right or wrong with this question. This is to judge your behavioral characteristics. Whether you let people be close, are you friendly enough and often this question is succeeded by questions like how will your best friend describe you.

Answer: I am very close to two people, who are my dearest friends, Sarah and Michelle. The three of us have been together for more than eighteen years now and have seen many ups and downs of life. We now live in different cities but we make the effort to stay in touch with each other.

Where do you see yourself in next five to ten years?

Tips: This is a chance to highlight your bright future and to portray yourself in the way you want to. Give the right answer so that it leaves no other choice for the employer but to hire you. Read about the most successful people in your career and following their footsteps try to come up with your own objectives. Try to answer this intelligently and bag this job before you walk out of the room.

Answer: In the next five years, I see myself being the best sales person this company ever had. I can go to any length to make sure that I achieve my goals successfully within time. I will work to becoming the best in my field by getting all the knowledge and training that my job requires. I am totally prepared to take on any challenge that comes across in performing my responsibilities.

What is your favorite animal and why?

Tips: Make an intelligent choice of an animal that has the best set of characteristics to support your job requirements. For example dolphin is intelligent and intuitive, lion is aggressive and dominating and elephant is strong and loyal.

Answer: My favorite animal is Elephant. I like him for his amazing strength and impressive loyalty which you seldom find in animal kingdom.

If in future you want to discontinue working for us, what would be the reason?

Tips: This question needs special attention and would require excellent diplomatic skills. You will want to stay and not leave as your research on this company shows that it fulfills all your requirements. You are not planning to leave so do not say that you will leave for a better opportunity.

Answer: I do not believe that switching companies is necessary for professional growth. I believe in loyalty. I wish to excel in my field and gain experience by working for this company.

What measures do you take to ensure balance between work life and family?

Tips: This question assesses your management skills. How well you maintain this balance shows how good you are at managing your priorities and how mentally organized you are.

Answer: Since I keep my priorities right, I know how to manage time well and being organized helps me keep this balance between professional life and personal life healthy.

Do you believe in taking risks?

Tips: The answer to this question depends on the job you are trying to get. If it involves taking risks then your answer should be according to that. In normal situations where risk taking is not encouraged, your answer should be that you are very cautious and avoid taking risky decisions.

Answer: I do not believe in taking unnecessary risks, but in some cases it becomes inevitable. Sometimes taking risks favors everybody, your company, you and others. A thorough analysis and careful planning can help taking risks a little less threatening.

Which activities take most of your free time?

Tips: The main idea behind asking this question is to know how healthy a life you have outside the professional one. If you lead a healthy life then the positivity will certainly help you be friendly and nice to colleagues. It also gives more stability to your personality. Loners and party fanatics are not the best options for this question.

Answer: I love watching TV with family, do some fun cooking at weekends and I play tennis with friends too.

Chapter 13: During The Interview -

Projecting the right image

During The Interview – Selling Yourself

In the previous sections, we have looked at how you can effectively prepare for the job interview including dealing with the tension leading up to and entering into the interview room.

You are well dressed with a good poise, have greeted your interviewer (s) correctly, created your comfortable sitting posture and you are now ready to convince your interviewer that you are the man or woman that they have been searching for to fill that job opening. To some the actual performance comes easily, for others they have to work at it. Some people are natural born sales people and know how to sell themselves others are not so lucky.

Generally speaking if you already work in a sales role, what will be explained next is really natural and it will be just a reminder of what you already know. Sales people are natural born performers whether it is due to their personality or due to the nature of the work they have previously carried out but the term "life is a stage and you are on it" has never spoken truer than at a job interview.

It all comes down to one thing and that is getting a stranger to believe in you and or your product. At an interview you are the product and you therefore need to put on a good performance.

There are many different qualities the interviewer is going to be looking for in their potential candidate which will encompass qualifications, experience, you as a person and the way that you integrate with others, your previous employment history, and your enthusiasm towards your career along with many, many other factors. So here are a few areas to consider – they are all really interlinked and if you can employ all of them at interview stage you are well on your way to getting that new job:

Show Your Interviewer That You Are Enthusiastic

So what exactly is the interviewer looking for? Well firstly I would say enthusiasm. If someone asks you a question and you give a one word answer it doesn't really look very enthusiastic. So the way to deal with this is to answer the question as deeply as you can.

For example; Interviewer "Your background is in sales but I see you are now involved in customer service" don't simply answer with a Yes or No answer, expand on it – so you could answer something along the lines of "Yes I was originally trained in sales, an area I spent several years working in which I thoroughly enjoyed. However I had the opportunity to expand my overall selling skills to encompass customer service so I jumped at the chance as I felt it would enhance my experience overall within my team".

Obviously you can tailor this to your own circumstances. Be enthusiastic don't just give one word or close ended answers, make your interviewer interested in you and what you have done, show him that you really are zealous about everything you do. To the interviewer this shows that you will be enthusiastic and dedicated should they decide to employ you.

Show Your Interviewer You Are a Confident Candidate And That You Know Your Stuff

Another area where all sales people are naturals is in confidence!

It is not always easy when you are under pressure and nervous to ooze confidence, but this is a really important area. The more confident you are the more chances you have of landing the job. Try and expand on your answers again in this area if you are asked a negative question try and respond with a positive confident answer.

For example; Interviewer "You don't appear to have done much cold calling for a while and this job will involve quite a large amount of self lead generation how do you feel about that" – you could answer along the lines of "Yes I haven't been involved in cold calling for 6 months which has been quite disappointing to me as I thoroughly enjoyed it and felt that it was one of my strong areas. I really have missed this element of my work because I got the opportunity of speaking to new people each day and I really got a high when I finally closed a deal that I new I had generated from scratch. Cold calling is an area I am keen to get back into and it's a talent that I feel comes naturally to me".

Show Your Interviewer That You Are Positive

I can tell a positive person the moment they utter a sentence! Can you say this about yourself? It's easy to become negative about anything in life but this attitude will get you nowhere in your career. In the work environment a positive person is a real asset to an employer.

Positive people give off positive vibes and those good vibrations nearly always rub off on other employees. The end result creates a happy, proactive, enthusiastic work force which ultimately creates a better working environment and more efficient team. If you can demonstrate this quality to your interviewer at interview stage you will definitely impress them.

Watching Your Body Language

Body language is an area that many interviewers will take seriously. What we do and how we do it can show underlying areas that do not have to be spoken to be picked up upon. Body language is an area that has been analysed for many, many years by professionals and interviewers alike and really is amazing what you can learn from someone just by their mannerisms. Just to give you an example - if you ask a person a question and their eyes gaze up thoughtfully to the left hand side of their eyeball you know that the chances of their answer being true are high. If on the other hand they look up to the right of their eyeball the chances are they are searching for a made up answer to your question! There are certain exceptions to the rule but the theory is based upon the fact that the left side of your brain is where you retrieve data from, the right, is the fictional side of your brain! Interesting isn't it and one to be aware of! Other areas that give off body language signals (without you knowing about them) are as follows:

Don't:

Crossing Your Arms: Makes you look defensive.

Sitting on the edge of your seat gives you away as being nervous.

Mess with your face or play with your jewelry or hair could mean you lack confidence or that you are hiding something.

Interrupt when being asked a question means that you have poor communication skills.

Give one word answers means you are not enthusiastic.

Do:

Smile as frequently as possible (especially when you are asked a question and respond to the person who has asked the question) but don't overdo it!

Keep your hands in your lap don't wave them around all over the place.

Keep eye contact at all times (I don't mean stare out your interviewer). If there is more than one interviewer flick from person to person.

Be articulate and listen carefully to each question before giving your answer.

Keep calm and don't panic!

Closing and Leaving The Interview

Towards the end of each interview, the interviewer will naturally ask you if you have any questions. At this point you can pop up the questions you have prepared. Be brief and to the point. This is not the time to ask about the pay package but rather ask about the short and long term goals of the company, the job etc. We will discuss more on this under the section on study of the tough questions.

Once the interview has finished the interviewer will offer closing remarks. Once this is done, you will stand, pick up your briefcase or handbag from under the chair (if that's where you put them) and shake hands with the interviewer (again in a firm but not grip wrenching manner!).

Try and avoid the temptation to wipe your sweaty hands on your clothes in front of the interviewer – a better tactic is to just clench your hands together and rub them a couple of times gently to remove any wetness.

Thank the interviewer for the time that they have afforded to you, say goodbye in a nice smiley manner and leave the room. Some people will escort you out onto the main floor others may see you out of the building but whichever try and stay as professional as possible – the jobs not yours until you have signed on the dotted line!

Chapter 14: Interview Grooming

You only get one chance to make a first impression. We've all heard that one. Before you even open your mouth to say "hello," you have already made an impression. You make your first impression with your appearance.

Do not wait until the morning of your interview to decide on what you will wear. Pick out your clothes the day before the interview. Dress as if you really want that job.

If you are going to work in an environment that is business or business casual, wear a business outfit to the interview. Err on the side of caution with business casual. Even though business casual is a little more dressed down version of business attire, don't chance their version of business casual being different from your version.

Women be conservative with your business outfit. Wear an outfit that makes you feel confident and professional. Wear a dark suit with pants or skirt (knee length). If the weather is extremely hot, it is understandable if you omit the jacket until right when you are walking into the interview. The colors should be black, dark grey, or navy. Less skin visible is better when it comes to tops. Wear close toe pumps or flats that matches the outfit if it's winter and open toe is alright to wear if it's hot like close to 90 degrees outside. Refrain from wearing stilettoes. No clear, neon colors, or anything remotely looking like shoes you would wear on a night out dancing at the hottest new club in town should be worn to an interview. Keep the jewelry simple and elegant. No dangling or jiggling earrings or bracelets. You want the interviewer to remember you, the person, and not what you wore to the interview.

Men be conservation with your business outfit. Also, wear a suit that will make you feel confident and keep your suits to colors such as black, dark grey, or navy. Please, no purple, brown, or neon color suits. It will be understandable for most positions if it's 90 degrees outside if you don't wear a jacket until you are about to walk through the door to the interview. Wear a tie that accessorizes your suit and not a tie that will draw attention to it. If you are not sure about a tie, don't wear that tie. Choose a tie to wear that is conservative. Make sure your shoes are polished and that they are one tone and one color. Do not wear multiple color shoes.

Does a casual job give you the right to wear whatever you want to the interview? No, it doesn't. Even if you are going on a job interview to flip burgers or to pack boxes, you should still dress as if you are trying your hardest to get hired. Do not wear blue jeans, t-shirts, sandals, and tennis shoes. Wear dress pants. Wear a button up shirt. Women can wear a dress that is at least knee length or skirt.

Hair should be groomed according to the position you are trying to obtain. Wearing a Mohawk is not a hairstyle for someone who is interviewing for a business or business casual dress company. It may be acceptable for someone who will be working outside or in a warehouse.

Although if you are interviewing to be a warehouse manager, a Mohawk is not a hairstyle that would be appropriate for the interview. Deciding whether to wear your hair down or pulled back is something you should play around with the day before your job interview.

The web site Pinterest has over 1,000 ideas for hair. Look at the different ways to groom your hair for a job interview.

Makeup should be polished and applied on more conservative for a job interview. You want everyone you encounter at the interview to remember you, the person, and not as the person wearing the reddest lipstick they've ever seen. This is one of those days that you should not be piling on the makeup heavy. Your powder and foundation should be natural to your skin tone. Refrain from overdoing the eye and lip liners. Do not double coat makeup around the eyes and lips. Lip gloss should lightly be applied and not having a very glossy appearance. Lightly apply on lipstick. If you wear blush, do a light dusting. If you need help with applying your makeup, visit a makeup counter at your local mall or ask a friend or family member to help you apply your makeup for the job interview.

Nail polish should be clear or a tone that does not draw attention to your nails. If you are not sure if your color will be too overpowering then wear clear polish. Hot pinks, orange, red, and neon colors should be avoided. Do not wear rhinestones on your nails or nail art to a job interview. Every finger should be polished the same color.

There are a few grooming matters that everyone needs to review before going to their next interview. Make sure your nails are trimmed and clean. Do not wear more than two earrings on each ear and remove other visible piercings unless you are interviewing for a job to do body piercings. Make sure your clothing is free of wrinkles. That means you may have to actually pull out an iron or visit a dry cleaners a few days before your interview. If you are not skilled at ironing, seek help from someone who is better skilled at ironing. Check your collar to make sure no tags are hanging from your suit or shirt and to make sure your collar does not need to be adjusted. Do not squirt perfumes and colognes directly on your clothes and no more than one squirt. You don't want everyone at the office, warehouse, etc. to smell you well after you have left the building. That's not the impression you want to leave with a company.

Chapter 15: Improving Your Job Application Results

Congrats! You're putting in the extra time and effort to truly help your application materials stand out from among the competition. Your application form is complete and flawless. Maintain your positive momentum by following through on the applications you submit, using the effective tips provided in this chapter.

Send a Second Submission

After you've applied to a potential employer, print a second, identical hardcopy version of your materials (cover letter, resume, and application form if the company requires it). Then, somewhere on your cover letter (the top-right corner is a good place) handwrite this message:

Second submission-I'm very interested

Send the materials with your handwritten note via snail mail to the employer. This simple step can significantly improve your chances of receiving a call for an interview. Why? When you send a hardcopy application, you set yourself apart from the crowd of electronic applicants.

Also, by submitting your materials more than one time (electronic and hardcopy, or two hardcopy versions), you increase your chances of being noticed. Your handwritten, "Second submission—I'm very interested" message shows that you're truly interested.

Make Follow-Up Calls

After you've sent two copies of your materials—the original and the second-submission version—make a note on your calendar to call in three business days to follow up. This will allow you to

• Confirm that your materials were received successfully (sometimes they don't make it to the intended recipient, especially if they were submitted electronically).

• Find out what will happen next in the hiring process.

• Make a personal connection with a screener.

Use these steps to follow up effectively:

1. Follow up three business days after you've sent your second submission.

2. Call the company and ask to speak to the hiring manager in charge of the position (whose name you should already know).

3. Communicate the following information, either directly to the individual, or on his or her voice mail: "Hello, this is YOUR NAME. I am calling regarding the POSITION TITLE currently open within your organization. I want to confirm that my application materials were received successfully, and also to find out more about what will happen next in your hiring process."

4. Include your phone number if you're leaving a voice-mail message, and mention that you sent a second set of materials, with a handwritten "Second Submission" message.

If you want to take your follow-up even further, call one week later, leaving a message like this:

Hello, NAME OF HIRING MANAGER. It's YOUR NAME, calling back to day that I'm still very interested in your opening, and I'm hopeful that I'll be called in for an interview. If it turns out that I'm not chosen, I wish you the best in finding the right person for the job, and please keep me in mind for future opportunities.

This leaves the hiring manager with a good impression of your interest and professionalism, as well as gives you peace of mind to know that you did a thorough job of following through.

Re contact Interesting Companies Six Months Later

Let's say that in January, you applied to the opening at Great Balls of Fire, Inc., a manufacturer of fireworks, and you love the idea of working for a business that makes things explode! You also sent a second submission, but didn't get called in for an interview. You're bummed, because it looked like a great position. Instead of writing off this opportunity forever, make a note on your calendar to recontact the hiring manager in June. Why? Because on average, 40 percent of individuals hired for a position don't work out within the first six months. Either they've already quit because the job wasn't right for them...or they've been fired because they weren't succeeding...or (and this is the most common scenario) they're still working at the job, but the boss isn't happy with their performance.

By following up six months later, you might connect with the hiring manager at the exact time that she's ready to make a change. Either call the hiring manager directly and let her know that you're still interested, or resubmit the materials (yes, a third submission!) that you sent originally, this time with a handwritten message stating that you are still very interested.

Use One Potential Employer to Lead You to Others

For example, let's imagine that the idea of working for Great Balls of Fire, Inc., really jazzes you. You love the idea of working for a fireworks manufacturer! So as soon as you've completed your first and second submissions to that company, take a few minutes to research other fireworks manufacturers, and then prepare materials (you can even reuse much of what you sent to the first company) to send to them, even if they don't have any advertised positions available.

This falls within the category of approaching companies directly and is extremely effective. Why? Because when a position opens at one company within an industry, it very often affects positions at other companies, as specialists shuffle from one company to another within that industry. Submitting a cover letter and resume directly to those other employers improves your chances of locating an opening before it ever gets advertised. Then, instead of competing against 100 other applicants, you would be the only one!

Why do you do it? Because, according to your brain, the opportunity is still open— it's a loose end that your mind needs to track. Yet instinctively you know that ruminating over unfulfilled job opportunities is a terrible waste of your time and energy.

So let's imagine a different scenario. Let's say, for instance, that you applied to a position that looked interesting, and instead of just cogitating on it day after day, you decide to do some follow-up. You print off and submit a hardcopy "second submission" package, an activity that takes you five minutes to complete. Three days later, you make a follow-up call (you call at 8 p.m. to reduce the chances of someone actually answering, but hey, you're calling!) and leave a message using the script provided in this chapter. This step took you three minutes. As a final follow-through activity, you leave a second message a week later, investing another three minutes of your time.

In total, you've invested 11 minutes of your time on highly productive follow-up activities and significantly improved your chances of being called in for an interview. But even more important, you've given your brain a reason to stop pondering about the opportunity over and over day after day, because it knows you've done your part to wrap things up, and you can let it go. That's why it's worth doing!

Follow up on applications you've submitted? Eek! For job seekers especially, this is a terrifying activity to consider doing. What if you get rejected? What if the hiring manager yells at you? What if some other horrible result happens? The "what ifs" surrounding follow-through can be endless and overwhelming. But instead of writing off the idea entirely, challenge yourself to experiment with small steps. Send a "second submission," or practice making a follow-up phone call. Like a muscle that rarely gets used, you might be pleasantly surprised to discover that once you begin, you can build your strength much easier, and less painfully, than you feared.

CHAPTER 16: THE INTERVIEW

At last the moment to shine at your interview arrives. The most important thing to keep in mind is to treat it like a conversation. In 1997 Steve Jobs interviewed James Green for a job at Pixar. When Green reflected back on that interview years later he noted that Jobs had him over to his home and "felt we had more of a conversation, than an interview."

A conversation is relaxed and friendly. It involves maintaining good eye contact, active listening, asking relevant questions based on information learned during the conversation, and answering the questions asked—not a running dialogue of your choosing.

The Questions

There are several standard questions most interviewers like to ask. While you can't be prepared for everything, there's nothing wrong about thinking and rehearsing the answers to some of these questions ahead of time.

Tell me about yourself?

This question is often used to gauge a little bit about your personality. When interviewers ask this question, they do not want your life story. They're usually looking for a brief answer with a hint of personality. This is the perfect time to mention a unique hobby you have, exotic trip you've taken, or some other piece of trivia about yourself. If you can relate it back to something to do with the job, all the better. But don't try too hard. If it's a stretch or just doesn't make logical sense, don't force the connection.

Tell me about a time when...?

Interviewers love to pull out questions that help them understand how you handle various situations. Some popular variations of this question include **when you displayed leadership skills, had to problem solve, or head a project.** Interviewers are less interested in the situation that lead up to action, than your response. Be honest and have a few situations at the ready should they ask.

Tell me a about a time you made a mistake and how you resolved the issue, what areas do you need to improve in?

These types of questions are also popular. While no one likes to talk about the areas they might come up short, don't dodge the question. The worst answer you can give an employer is to tell them you don't make mistakes or have any shortcomings. All humans fail and can stand to improve in something. Insisting you're perfect or have no issues is dishonest. It also implies you're not open to change or growth. Or worse yet, you may not be willing to take direction. Interviewers seldom want employees who don't listen or are unwilling to take direction.

While you want to give an honest assessment of your capabilities, you don't have to sell yourself short either. There's no need to share the worst thing that ever happened to you at a job or talk about an incident that may have gotten you fired. Pick something truthful, but not necessarily detrimental. Even better, if you can include a key lesson or something of importance that was learned from the mistake or shortcoming, all the better.

Bill Gates notes, "It's fine to celebrate success, but it's more important to heed the lessons of failure."

Doing so displays honesty, an aptitude for growth, flexibility, and possibly an empathy for others that might experience similar situations.

Where do you see yourself in 5 or 10 years?

Elon Musk is known for asking this question along with one other. There are many right answers to this question and one absolutely wrong answer. Unless you are interviewing to be groomed to take over the interviewer's position, never ever tell the interviewer you hope to have their job in a few years. Most interviewers don't want to hire someone who will make them watch their backs at all times. It's also rather presumptuous if not insulting to tell someone that you could do their job just as well as they could, without on the job training or earning your time.

How would you change this company *or* what have you seen that you think could be improved here?

While many interviewers applaud innovative ideas, they also appreciate tact. It's all right to share your ideas. It's not all right to trash the organization in the process. A good critic doesn't criticize everything. Instead he or she reflects in an issue and supplies a positive solution. One of the best ways to tactfully deliver a critique is to sandwich it between positive statements.

One: Start by focusing on some strengths of the organization. "I really like the way X Corp makes each customer feel like an individual by calling them by their names."

Two: Talk about the shortcoming. If you can describe it as something that needs improvement all the better. "I think X Corp could really improve on the way it collects money from customers."

Three: Provide your solution and explain how it might improve the situation. "I think X Corp might see improved sales if you were to offer an online pay option. I think clients might like the convenience of paying on the spot instead of mailing their bills or stopping by to pay."

Four: Conclude with another positive statement as well as the likely positive outcome. "It's great the way X Corp treats everyone like family. No doubt that's why you have so many repeat customers. Adding the online option will not only keep them coming back, but help X Corp bring in more invoices on time."

Suggesting improvements or changes using positive sandwiches is a diplomatic, non-threatening way to convey new ideas, without seeming presumptive, coming off like a know it all, or a corporate climber gunning for the interviewer's job.

Why do you feel you would be a good fit for this job, or why do you want to work for us?

This seems pretty straightforward. While it's all right to tell an interviewer that this is your dream job or something you've hoped to do all your life, interviewers want to hear something bigger than you. They want to hear why your skills are perfect for their organization. Make sure your answer reflects more about how you will be an asset and benefit to them, than how they will help you. Use fewer "I" statements and more "you" statements.

Do you have any questions for me/us?

This is the other question Elon Musk likes to ask. Shaking your head or answering that you think an interviewer has covered everything may seem like the polite or complimentary thing to do, but please this is the time to ask any follow-up questions. If an interviewer asks this question, he or she really wants to know if there is anything else they can share. Asking a question or questions shows that you were actively listening, interested in what they have to say, aren't afraid to speak up, inquisitive, and curious. All of those are great qualities, especially for a growing organization. It is best to have at least one question at the ready to display your soft skills as well as to convey interest and a willingness to engage or collaborate.

Is there anything else you would like to add?

This is your last chance to impress, your closing sales pitch. Always add something else. Restate what benefits you would bring to their organization. It could be something you feel is important that the interviewer didn't ask, something you feel he or she misunderstood that needs clarification, or a quick summary of you and your work experiences. Don't be afraid to ask for the job if it feels right.

Chapter 17: Types of Interviews

There are different types of interviews that you may experience while searching for a job. Before you begin to feel frustrated, let's educate ourselves. You may experience informational interviews, phone/screening interviews, individual interviews, group interviews, and panel interviews. It is important to know the interview process by asking the recruiter or hiring manager. In addition, understanding the differences between each type of interview will allow you to be better prepared.

Informational Interview

Informational interviews are taken by job seekers from experienced personnel of a particular field. This type of interview is also known as an open house interview. The goal is for the job seeker to learn more about a particular position, employer, or industry. It is a great opportunity to ask for advice and takes notes. Learning more about a particular position, employer, or industry will allow you to know the in's and out's to be better informed when it comes time to making a decision. This type of interview varies in length. It usually depends on how many candidates the hiring manager or recruiter needs to talk with, and how much time they are interested in spending with you. If they spend more time talking to you than others, it's usually a good sign. Although you want to ask plenty of questions and learn more, it doesn't end there. This is also an opportunity to network, not only with professionals in that field but with other job seekers as well.

Telephone Interview

If the interview process is at least 2 or 3 rounds, chances are the first interview will be conducted over the phone. Also known as a screening interview, it is a cost effective way for the employer to screen candidates for a position. This type of interview usually lasts anywhere between 15 – 45 minutes. Phone interviews are similar to an open book exam. Since you will be communicating over the phone, you can have the job description, notes, and additional information in front of you, without the interviewer knowing. The interviewer will not be able to see your body language, so it is a lot less stressful than an in-person interview. When speaking and responding to questions, give refined and positive answers using an energetic tone. This will allow the interviewer to hear your excitement about the position.

Similar to telephone interviews, employers may even ask for a Skype interview or an interview over a web cam. This will allow the interviewer to view your body language, so make sure to brush up on those skills if needed.

Individual Interview

An individual interview is the most common type of interview, so make sure to master this. Also known as a "one on one", this type of interview is usually conducted regardless of how many rounds the process takes. It is a one on one interaction between you and the interviewer that usually makes the job seeker more nervous than any other type of interview. Body language will be noticed in this type of interview, and it could be the difference maker when choosing from their top candidates. The individual interview process usually takes anywhere between 30 minutes to 2 hours. A shorter interview will require you to be more concise and impactful with your answers. A longer interview will allow you to go further into detail using specific examples to illustrate your response. It is important to know the duration of the interview prior to interviewing, to allow you to prepare accordingly.

Group Interview

Group interviews contain multiple candidates. This is usually held when hiring multiple candidates for the same position. It is another cost effective way for the employer to screen candidates. These interviews are lengthy, and usually take anywhere between one to two hours. Sometimes the interviewer will allow each candidate to answer the same question, or sometimes they will choose someone to answer based on a raise of hands. It is important that you react quickly if the interviewer does not allow everyone to answer each question, but even more important to think your response through before answering. You want your voice to be heard, but quality is much more important than quantity.

Panel Interview

A panel interview involves the candidate interviewing with multiple hiring managers at the same time. This allows you the opportunity to impress multiple decision makers. This type of interview typically occurs during the final stages of interviewing. Some candidates find it difficult to engage with each member of the hiring team. When you are responding to questions, make eye contact with each interviewer in the room, not just with the person who asked the question. Aim to develop rapport with as many members of the team as possible. Doing so, will put you at ease with each hiring manager and will allow yourself to feel comfortable.

Chapter 18: The Panel Interview!

"Whenever you're asked if you can do a Job, tell them, "Certainly I can!" Then get busy and find out how to do it."——Theodore Roosevelt

It's hard enough having to walk into a hiring manager's office for an interview that your entire future seems to rely on. What happens when you have to meet an entire panel of 4, 5, or even 6 people? Well, you can imagine how much more the nerves will act up in that kind of scenario. Not being prepared and not having your nerves under control would be a recipe for disaster. You're going to have to deal with a mixture of emotions from different sources. Winning over the majority of the panel is vital, anything less than that would likely mean failure to land that job. However, there are ways to make the most of that situation and turn it around for your own benefit.

Why A Panel Interview:

Panel interviews are preferred in certain organizations for a variety of reasons:

A panel interview helps the organization save time and costs associated with holding serial interviews. Every member of any department associated with the job description gets the chance to ask questions and assess your suitability for the role.

Panel interviews are perceived to be fairer and more objective than single-person interviews because a broader range of opinions are taken into consideration before choosing the successful candidates.

The panel interview is seen as an opportunity to examine how a candidate copes with higher levels of stress. It is also an opportunity to see how the candidate manages to interact with a variety of individuals with different areas of core competencies.

The interview is seen as being more detailed and more rigorous because a successful candidate would have been able to satisfactorily answer questions from experts in different areas of expertise.

Who'll be included on the panel?

The panel will typically include all relevant specialists related to the job responsibilities in question. This could be anywhere from two to eight individuals. One trick to getting ahead of the competition in the panel interview is finding out which individuals would be most likely to be included. You might ask "How exactly am I supposed to do that? " It's certainly simpler than it might seem. You could simply call human resources of the interviewing organization and there's a high probability that you'll get the required information. Most companies do not have any rules against giving that sort of information to the public. If that fails another simple but more tedious method would involve using social media to your advantage, particularly LinkedIn.

When you do succeed in gathering enough information on the most likely individuals to be on the panel, take advantage and know these people inside out. Study their backgrounds, hobbies and areas of expertise; doing this will give you more of a chance of building a personal connection with these individuals when the interview comes begins. They'll certainly not be able to help being impressed with your thoroughness.

The key to being a hit at the panel interview is to be as relaxed as possible. The average candidate will be a bundle of nerves. If you manage to keep calm, you'll have already made a big impression. The other thing that you should definitely be doing as soon as the interview starts is building a personal connection with as many members of the panel as possible. This is where doing your research on each individual will really come in handy.

Tips to come out tops in the panel interview:

Make a Grand Entrance

I cannot say this enough, getting the introductions right are vital to your performance at a panel interview. As soon as you step into that room, you should work on making a positive impact on every one of the panelists. It will set the tone for the rest of the interview. Getting it wrong might just be fatal to your chances of being successful at the interview. Be sure to spend some time engaging in small talk with as many of the panelists as possible. There might not be enough time to meet everyone on that level but the more you succeed in engaging the brighter your chances at pulling off a winning performance during the interview. When you're introduced to each member of the panel, don't forget the importance of a firm handshake. Shake hands firmly and be sure to make eye contact coupled with a slight smile. Do this with every member of the panel. Be sure to use names when you're greeting each member. It's also important to take each introduction slowly and deliberately, rushing through the introductions might be perceived as a sign of nervousness.

Always take notes:

Your note-taking skills are crucial at a panel interview. It's hard enough putting thoughts together and remembering all the questions with one interviewer, imagine what it could be like having to handle a panel of eight. But there is a proper way to do it though, or else taking notes might just seem rude. As soon as you're asked to have a seat, politely ask if they mind you take notes during the interview. The answer is likely to be no, go ahead and take out your notepad and pen. The first things you should have down are the names of your interviewers. You should handle each question by addressing each interviewer by name. This simple act establishes a connection and marks you out as an organized individual with great communication skills.

Prepare for the Panel's Questions:

Just like in the single interview person interview every question should be addressed from the perspective of what you bring to the role and the company. In a panel interview, you must be aware that each panelist will ask questions from their unique perspective in reference to their backgrounds and roles within the company. Here again, the amount of research on each of the panelists will really be useful.

Be aware of your communication:

Because the interview panel is composed of a number of people and not just one, it is safe to expect that they would come from diverse backgrounds. Being clear in your spoken communication is important so that everyone will understand your answers despite any cultural differences. The manner in which the question is answered is also important. When you answer a question, make eye contact with the person who asked the question. As you proceed to answer the question, scan each of the faces of the members of the panel, making eye contact and stopping briefly on each face. Return to the person who initially asked the question as you conclude your answer.

As it has been mentioned earlier, answer each question while remaining as calm and composed as possible. Breathe cleanly and deeply to calm any nerves while paying attention to the questions being asked. One tactic that really makes a big impression with panelists is when you can connect two questions asked by two different panelists and address them at once while making reference to the other question. For example saying something like "That's a great observation Andy; the scenario is a similar one to Fred's question only with slightly different dynamics..."

Ask the Right Questions:

Asking the right questions when it's time for you to do the asking can only boost your chances of making a lasting impression on the minds of interview panelists. Use your carefully built up knowledge of the company as well as the panelists to ask questions that are thoughtful and intelligent. The questions should have been prepared beforehand and should be addressed to the appropriate members of the panel while taking their organizational roles into consideration.

Close the Interview:

At the end of the interview, you can make an even bigger closing statement by asking in the simple question "Is there anything else you would like me to provide information on?" Allow your eyes to roam across the face of each panels, make sure there's plenty of eye contact. Shake hands firmly again with each individual before leaving the room and be sure to thank each person personally for the opportunity. Again, remember to address each individual by their names.

Chapter 19: What To Do If You Get The Job

Now that the perfect resume and cover letter have been submitted, and that rigorous interview is over, at the end of all your efforts, research, and professional presentation, are you really all that surprised that you got the long-awaited call, and the job is yours. What a spectacular feeling it is to know that all the time, energy, and efforts you put into the ongoing application and interviewing process have all paid off. However, before you accept that "perfect" job, there are a few small details you want to take care of before walking into your new place of employment, and embracing your new job.

Guidelines To Follow After You Land The Job

1. Get An Offer of Employment Letter - Before actually accepting your new position, reach out to your new employer and ask to have all the details of the job

put into a formal employment offer letter. Typically, this type of letter will include your title, supervisor, start date, insurance benefits, 401K information, PTO time, salary, hours of employment, and any particulars with regard to commissions, overtime, or travel time, if applicable. Whether you obtain the information in a hard copy letter form or email matters not, just as long as you have all the stipulations and terms of your new job in writing. Many companies will present the new employee with a written offer letter that requires signatures on the part of both parties, confirming all the agreed upon terms.

2. A Final Pre-Employment Meeting - It's a good idea to have one more meeting with the human resource personnel prior to your start date to allow you the opportunity to discuss any last minute details, or concerns you may have. At this final meeting, it might be wise to ask for some insight on your immediate supervisor or manager, and perhaps ask questions about the overall office

environment, dress code, and work atmosphere.

3. Negotiate Your Salary Terms - Unless you agreed on a set salary during the interviewing process, once your employment offer is made you can certainly make an effort to negotiate a salary that is both reasonable and acceptable to you. Many candidates are completely unaware that when a potential new employer simply makes mention of a specific salary in casual preliminary conversations, there is room, more often than not, for a higher negotiated salary that has typically been budgeted for in anticipation of such a request.

4. Take a Few Days To Process - If you find yourself even slightly hesitant about accepting the job offer, for whatever reason it may be, then thank the human resource personnel for making the offer to you, and request that they allow you a few days to process it all, and think it over. If you are having any doubts at all, you do not want to accept the position only to find out that two weeks into it you are

unhappy with your decision. This would be remarkably unfair to yourself, and to the company as well as your new coworkers.

5. Pay Attention to Your Inner Self - If you are the type of person who typically follows their own instincts and looks to your inner self for confirmation, and you find yourself thinking that something is just not in line, or just doesn't seem right about the new job offer, then follow your own instincts. If you are experiencing these types of feelings following a job offer, then rest assured there is something out of whack, and you should reconsider accepting the offer at this time.

6. Sign On the Acceptance Line - If after all the above formalities have been addressed and met, you find yourself feeling both excited and confident about your new job offer and the company you are about to begin your employment with, then don't waste a moment longer. Go ahead. Sign on the acceptance line, date your offer letter, and enjoy the sense of accomplishment you are feeling as you begin the next leg of your career journey.

Many candidates make the simple mistake of being too hasty, and lose sight of the important details during this time of excitement and celebration. If you give attention to the guidelines discussed above, you are sure to find yourself fully engaged in your new position with a complete understanding of all the terms of your employment agreement, and all the expectations the company has for you. Understanding these important elements will eliminate any disappointments or frustrating surprises during the early weeks of your employment. Having all the cards on the table upfront is a sure fire formula for a happy and successful transition to your new company and your new job. The entire job seeking and interviewing process was truly challenging, but in the end, your dedication and determination paid off. You are now the proud new employee of the company, and recognized by all as the newest member of the team!

Chapter 20: Nailing A Phone Interview

One of my favorite forms of interviews to give is a phone interview. I can really be myself and I don't have to shroud my facial expressions when I hear uproarious answers to questions I've asked. Vice versa, a phone interview should be your ticket to shine. The phone is a great tool that helps filter many distracting self-conscious thoughts. There are fewer opportunities to stir these emotions that the sometimes-intimidating vision can bring. You don't have to make eye contact, and best of all, I can't see you sweating profusely as you think about professional ways to vaunt about your accomplishments. Phone interviews are one of the best ways to ensure you get an invitation for an in-person face-to-face interview.

While studying in undergrad, I worked at a radio station and did voice over work as a side source of income. I currently reside in California and like to practice voice acting as a hobby, hopefully to one day narrate movie trailers and documentaries professionally. One thing that voice acting has taught me, is how to use my voice to draw in an audience to a particular story, product, or service. When having a phone interview, you must become a voice actor. You don't necessarily have to have golden LaFontaine pipes or do impressions, but you should know how to capture the listener's attention by controlling your pitch, volume, inflection, speed, and all the things a voice actor would think about when reading a script.

Good phone skills also take good listening skills. You have to remember that you are not the one directing the conversation when having a phone interview. However, you are guiding it. The goal is simple. You are trying to develop the phone interview into a face-to-face in-person interview. You want to be professional, conversational, and just charming enough to make me, as the recruiter, want to meet and see what you present like in person. Basically, will you be a good culture fit or not?

A good phone interview, matched with the right skills and experience, will always lead to an in-person interview. So just like talking on the phone to someone you're attracted to, your goal should always be to sound appealing. You should speak clearly and concisely, making sure you are cognizant of if you're talking too fast or slow, and if you're coming across friendly and professional. Practice talking to friends and family members about your professional background over the phone. Get comfortable talking in different settings and learn how to guide phone conversations, highlighting your accomplishments, without doing all the talking or sounding condescending.

Chapter 21: Person attending interview for the first time in life

This is a different situation than what we discussed in early chapters. We should understand a fresher's heart beat is faster than others when attending an interview. The person has no previous experience. In such case, we have to coach him / her for the interview. To such situations framing of the interview has to be carefully tailored. Interview should be mainly based on educational qualifications, candidates extra activities in school, other social activities and general knowledge.

Candidate has to take some extra efforts to develop or memorize above mentioned aspects. Thinking that I am fresher, person should not be lazy. Every body has talents, skills and fresh ideas. You must sharpen your knowledge with available resources. You have to think very positive. An interview board always interviews a person who is attending interview for the first time in a very soft and smooth manner. Some times they may help you to answer to their questions. There is nothing to get funk. As described in an early chapter it's necessary to concern on dress code, neatness, being polite to interview board, smartness and professionalism.

Exchanging ideas, getting advise and doing some rehearsal interviews with senior members is of immense importance to a new comer. Through coaching we can develop the person's personality. You must face interview in a relaxed mood, smartness and professional look will add values to the person's personality. The manner of answering questions has to be taught properly. Getting advises from professional people who conduct interviews, if anybody in the vicinity can direct you towards the success. Normally you have to answer some questions as given below.

Can you please introduce yourself?

What you have been doing straight after finishing your higher studies?

Some thing about your family background?

What are your ambitions & targets in life?
What type of a profession do you enjoy?
Any extra curricular activities in school?
Can you brief about that literature association you were involved in?
Do you wish to join as a trainee with a monthly paid training allowance or are you interested of a permanent employment?
If you are seriously looking for an opportunity to get into some occupation, you have to answer the above questions very sensibly. They have asked you all normal questions that you could have answered alright. Look at the last question there; this is actually a simple test they give you to judge your attitude. Although the question looks simple, it has some deepness to consider. They try to test you, whether you are job oriented or money oriented. When you say that you wish to join as a trainee, promptly they will be impressed on you. There is a hidden indication in your answer that you like to be groomed within company for future prospects.

Study about an interview – important to job seekers and beginners

I thought it's advisable to discuss about objectives of interviews with new comers. Interview can be considered as an energy bargain. Candidates attend interviews to bargain on their knowledge, education, energy and precious time. In the meantime companies try to hire their so called resources to fulfill their industrial or business requirements; whatever it is. You attempt to secure the vacant job by attending to an interview; there you face with a competition because all other candidates have the same intention. Even without any previous experience or job knowledge some succeed interviews. How is that? Those are the people who understand bargaining & hiring in job market.

Employees of organizations have their own rights in any capacity whether trainees or permanent cadres. They are called employee rights. For example employer is bound to pay you a salary, other benefits as per the terms of their appointment letters. Employees always can fight for rights, in case of abuse by employer. As well they have some obligations towards the employer and organization as per their employment conditions, where they have agreed upon. When the employee obligations are not full filled, employer can take suitable disciplinary action on them. All newly joined employees and job seekers should determine to act accordingly.

Employees engaged in employments have some knowledge and experience about these issues but As HR professionals it's our duty to enlighten younger generations about conditions of employment and its environmental behaviors. Then only we can expect a smooth running employment/ industrial relations. If the younger generation is properly trained and coached, we can minimize global industrial disputes. That will help to enhancement of productivity as well the development of employee welfare. To meet expected achievements, organizations have to implement "Training & Development" programs as per their own requirements. When the above operations are streamlined, we can see how easy to manage organizations and harvest best reaps of their plough.

Some valuable material to coach new employees.

This training material is equally advantageous to persons attending interviews for the first time. I have done so many researches to prepare this as a work shop to above mentioned categories of employees and participants in interviews.

Questionnaire

1. (a) Who is the employer?

(b) Who is an employee?

(c) How do you orient a new employee in your department?

2. How do you educate an employee about his / her work responsibilities, Company Expectations, obligations and general rules of the company?

3. How do you evaluate work performances of trainees and probationers?

4. What steps do you adopt to control absenteeism?

5. How do you identify a misconduct of an employee?

6. When an employee commits an act of misconduct, what steps do you take to correct
the employee?

7. How do you response when your employees are unhappy in work place?

8. To avoid labor unrest in your department, what precaution measures do you take?

9. As line managers how do you co-operate with HR Department in developing Industrial relations activities?

10. Give your suggestions to improve Employer / Employee relationship in the company?

We give below a set of answers to above questionnaire for you to understand the situations.

Answers

(a) Those who employ work men. A body of employers (a company) that employs work men.

Those who employ workmen on behalf of another person.

(b) Those accepted a written agreement to work under an employer.

Those who agree and work on a certain contract in any capacity either the contract is expressed in writing or implied.

Whose services have been terminated but (until the termination is legally Justified).

(c) It is extremely important to give a warm welcome to new recruits to make them feel comfortable in the new working environment.

Introduce new employee to all the employees in the section individually and show the work area of the new employee.

2. Provide the person with a job description, stating all job functions that he / she should perform, obtain the person's signature on the duplicate and introduce that to his personal file.

Educate the new recruit about the work responsibilities, company expectations and about obligations towards company. Also general principles and work schedules.

3. In the first instance all new recruits including probationers and trainees must be informed of their work responsibilities and company procedures.

Their attendance, work performances, punctuality and behavior must be very closely observed. There should be an appraisal system to evaluate their performances. New recruits must be advised verbally or in writing as per the situations.

4. Employees should be educated about leave enlightenment, procedure of applying leave. It is necessary to pre plan work in the section and holding person responsible for work assigned.

It's extremely important to educate employees constantly that absenteeism directly effects to poor productivity, disorganize of routine work, wastage and excessive over time. Also it's important to enlighten them about the impact on individual's personal records due to absenteeism. Employees should be educated about the consequences of not reporting for work without informing.

5. Sabotage, negligence of duties, insubordination, working under influence of liquor, misappropriation of funds, habitual no pay leave, willful damage to company property etc. can be identified as misconducts.

When misconduct is reported, the department head or immediate supervisor should take first action by issuing the person verbal or written warning. All these warnings have to be properly recorded in member's personal file.

6. If the same person is found repeating of misconducts, definitely he should be warned severely in writing of which a copy should be sent to his personal file.

When it is a misconduct that should be dealt seriously, Head of department has to report to HR department with immediate effect.

7. It's great to find out all reasons behind causing them to be unhappy. This can be done by talking them privately and organizing internal meetings.

Head of departments and immediate superiors should try to find solutions within the departments and failing, they have to report to HR department and top management.

8. Take all possible steps to build up a pleasant environment to for them to work make necessary arrangements to build up a friendly / homely relation ship among employees to co-operate with each other and build up a good team spirit.

9. Follow up with correct Industrial relation practices and employment / labor regulations. Stream line information systems, internal communication practices enabling all company communication transparent.

Encourage top & middle management to set examples to new recruits. Culture and discipline should be monitored from head to foot in an organization

The above questionnaire and answers can be conducted in any organization in a forum that new recruits, trainees and probationers gather. It is most important to conduct this in a form of a work shop. HR professionals can make best use of this work shop to enlighten the new employees, how they should behave and attend to their work responsibilities.

We can do lots of case studies based on the above process. It should never be nature of a lecture. We must get new recruits' participation in this program. You have to allow them to ask questions, express their fresh ideas and any new things to add as proposal. Then only this work shop will be employee related and results oriented.

This work shop will be very important to persons who intend attending interviews for first time, job seekers after completing studies and people who have failed in interviews. Anybody going through and practicing this questionnaire will add extra values to them and definitely they will get through interviews very easily.

At this stage now we have discussed about most of the areas that will help you to gain a sound knowledge, how to prepare for an interview, how to face an interview and various stages of interviews. Also we have discussed about frequently asked questions in interviews. This is fundamental information, questions and answers will vary in accordance with employment sectors but all will be based on same principle. Don't forget interviews are held to select best people.

Great tips for job interviews

In an interview listening is a great factor all candidates should concern about. When you enter interview room your mind must be free of other irritating thoughts.

Example: Take two jugs, one with three quarter filled with water and other is absolutely empty. Get water filled to a similar size jug, we will number the jugs as 1, 2 & 3 respectively. Now empty the jug 3 to jug 1, which is already three quarter filled. You will find water overflowing from jug 1, Once again fill jug 3 with water and pour in to jug 2. That jug has the capacity to contain entire water volume of jug 3 you will notice no overflowing of water.

In the same manner enter interview arena with pure mind. That will help you to a great extent to understand what they ask. As your mind is free from other thoughts, every thing they ask will pour in to your mind, like how we emptied water in jug 3 to jug 2. I assume that you have got this clearly.

Make sure you are in relaxed mind, well prepared for the interview, smart, neatly dressed to give a professional look. It is important that you keep all your documents, certificates & work samples if any, to an order. When they ask for any documents you should not struggle or get exited. Struggling and excitement denotes that you are a disorganized character. You have to be energetic over the interview desk. Do not yawn, if you want to cough please excuse and do so. It's always better to keep away from those misbehaviors. As you enter wish them to interview board by shaking hands, then introduce yourself to them. Normally it is a decent practice that interview board introduce themselves to the interviewees. If they do not adopt that practice, you don't make it an issue.

If you feel that they apply some pressure on you, just keep normal because you are now armed with all great interview tips /

hints etc. They may apply hard sometimes to test you. Attention to detail, good listening and good manners will add values to your personality in an interview. If they ask some thing wrong or irrelevant, you may decently say that is wrong or irrelevant. Put that to them in a sober manner. They will finally decide that you are intelligent, knows the job well. At any rate do not nod your head as answers, unless you are dumb. Also under any circumstances you should not turn interview to an unpleasant argument or to a dispute. When they do not agree with you on certain things, you can produce facts, data and proof to say that you are correct. Then they have to accept your explanations.

There can be instances that some member of the interview board answering telephone calls, when interview is in progress or similar things of that nature. How you should act / behave in such a situation? Please take no notice of those things. It's their privacy; you have nothing to do with. We have taught you in an early chapter, how you should enter interview room. In an interview every candidate may have some verifications get cleared and some important information to know. Please do not rush for that information. Normally before the end of interview, they will give you a time to ask anything that you want to know. Then it's your turn to ask or verify things. If they do not give you a chance you can always excuse and put forward your questions.

At the end of the interview again you have to thank the interview board by shaking hands. When you come out from the room position your chair properly in the same position as it was.

Common questions in an interview

In an interview they will like know your living styles also. One may think that is personal to members, no an organization will like to recruit people of good culture, well organized people and persons with sober habits. They will round up you putting some questions about your family background, your associates and friends. They might ask how you spend your leisure time or similar questions. If you give satisfactory answers, you will be automatically lifted to a high standard. For example we will give you some specimen questions.

What made you to apply for this job position?

Why do you think that this company is a better company comparing to your company?

In average how many hours you work for a week? Are you paid over time to extra hours you perform?

Other than the salary what are other cash & non cash benefits you enjoy at present job?

If we place you on the same salary, with a company maintained vehicle do you accept?

Why did you depart from previous job?

What's the employee strength of your present company?

If I ask can you brief about your company turn over per annum and profit / loss margin?

How do you like our company & staff?

Will your employer release you in a calendar month?

Your success in interview will be based on your job competency, presenting to interview, experience, qualifications, how developed & organized are you and salary terms agreed upon. Remember that you are on a competition because all other candidates try everything possible to secure the job. Another area is checking of your reference.

You must name good referees, like to recommend you. Some employers hand over the process of reference checking to HR department, then HR manager will do the reference check solely over the phone. I know there are some companies they ask for references / recommendations under confidential cover by mail. When they are asked to submit recommendation on writing always that will be a lengthy report.

Chapter 22: During the Interview

The Basics

Now we are getting ready to get to the interview. We have done our preparations, we have practiced the most common questions and we have done a few practice interviews as well. We know all about the company, their competition and all the other important information we should know and we're all set to go.

So now all we need is to go over a few things that might seem like common sense but still are mistakes many people make because they just weren't thinking or because they just didn't feel it made much of a difference. Whatever the reasons might be, be aware of the following so that you make the best impression you possibly can.

Be On time

You are looking for someone to give you a job. A job where you will be expected to be reliable and show up on time every single day unless you have a good reason for being late. Don't start off on a negative by not arriving on time for your interview. Unless you have a good reason, and this is communicated to the right people ahead of time, this could throw you right out of the running.

Give yourself extra time and take traffic into consideration as well as the weather. Plan on arriving at least a half hour before your interview. You can always sit in the car and read a book or go for a cup of coffee. But you want to be where you are supposed to be at least 15 minutes early ready and willing to go.

Be Nice

Contrary to what some people think, nice people generally do better than nasty or surly people. People who get along with others are generally preferred over the entitled obnoxious full of themselves type of person.

Personality and demeanor are two things that are very important in an interview. The interviewer is going to want to see that you are skilled enough to do the job and nice enough to fit in well with your coworkers. Come up short in either category and you probably won't get the job.

Look Nice

I realize that appearance is just on the outside and doesn't necessarily speak to the kind of person you are or how skilled a worker you can be. But how you look is a critical part of the first impression people make of you. Most of the time they see you before speaking to you so it is in your best interest to look the way people in that job expect you to look.

If you have a problem with people judging you by your appearance you have every right to feel that way and to look however you want to look. But as we already have said it is up to you to impress them not for them to accept whatever you want them to accept. The decision is your and yours alone.

But if you insist on going to that financial planner interview with 14 facial studs and four nose rings to go along with the purple hair and the 74 tattoos, don't be devastated when you are not chosen for the position. There are choices to be made and we live with the consequences of those choices.

Appropriate attire might be professional attire or business causal depending on the interview and position. Personally I advise men to wear a suit or at least a jacket and tie and women to wear a nice dress. This is regardless of the position you are applying for. Proper attire shows respect for the company and the interviewer as well as a commitment on your part towards the position.

Be Courteous

You should be courteous all through your life but especially to everyone you speak to when you come in for your interview. And by everyone I mean everyone. Some companies will make you wait for a while and then ask the receptionist how you were while you were waiting. Did you sit there patiently or did you complain and stare impatiently. Sometimes every part of the visit from the time you walk in until the time you walk out is watched and scripted for a purpose.

Be Positive

Interviewers LOVE positive people. Spend the interview making nothing but positive statements. Tell them what you can do and what you have done. Don't waste time telling them what you can't do or talking negatively. If they ask you about something negative do your best to turn it into a positive by the end of the answer.

Turn mistakes into learning lessons and hopefully have examples where learning from a mistake helped you do better in the future. Eliminate negative words and phrases and make everything as positive as possible. Almost everyone likes positive people better than negative ones. That includes co-workers as well which is why this matters so much.

Be Confident & Strong

Interviewers love people who are confident in who they are and in their skills and abilities. They want people who are not afraid to make a decision or to speak their mind. They do not want someone so insecure that they won't do a thing unless someone approves it in advance.

The most productive people in this world are the ones who are not afraid to take action quickly when they know what the right thing to do is. Indecision costs time and money and can also result in lost opportunities and customer dissatisfaction.

Keep in mind, though, the while interviewers love confidence and strength, they do not like obnoxious or arrogant people. Do not come off as thinking you are better than anyone else even if you might feel that way. Explain your accomplishments without bragging. Discuss your successes without boasting. Show your strengths with humility and reserve. In other words, let your actions and accomplishments speak for themselves at least some of the time.

Show Passion!

Too many people approach a job opportunity as a way to get a bigger paycheck or an extra week's vacation. But those motivators work for just a short period of time. Once you become used to the larger paycheck and the extra time off the real problems of the job soon resurface. This is something that recruiters and Human Resource people are well aware of.

What they want to see from their applicants is a passion for the opportunity and the company. They want to see people who have researched the company and know what the job is inside and out. They want to hear ideas the applicants have about how they can help makes things better and help the company grow.

In other words they want people who are thinking about the job first and the paycheck second. Whether or not that is reasonable is debatable but for now let's give them what they want to see and sort out the rest later!

Ok, those are a few of the basics when it comes time for you interview. Now let's switch gears a bit and discuss what attitudes you should have as you walk through the door. Because attitudes have everything to do with presentation and your interview is just one big presentation with you on center stage.

Here are a few things you should consider when it comes to how you react and behave during your interview:

Be a Problem Solver

The job you are being interviewed for exists because of certain needs and certain problems. You need to look at your approach in this interview as being the world's best problem solver. You need to show the interviewer and the company how you are able and capable of solving their problems.

Chances are at some point you will be interviewed by the manager of the department you will be working in. what better way to interview with that person than telling him how hiring you will reduce the problems that make it across his or her desk every day. Imagine the impression you would make as you explain to him how hiring you would make his own job easier and less stressful.

Can you think of a better way to get someone to hire you? I can't.

Think Like the Hiring Manager

Much along the same lines, know who is interviewing you and their position in the company. Usually they will give you that information in their introduction. Then address every answer to every question in the way someone in that position wants to hear it. Make the answers as personally relevant as they possibly can be.

If you are interviewing with your future department head, answer each question with how what you would do would make their department better, more productive and higher functioning. Make them aware that a better operating department would mean less stress for the manager.

Talk about every one of your skills and accomplishment in ways that make it obvious as to how they would benefit their department and the company. No generic statements but instead highly targeted and pointed statements designed to impress the interviewer in his or her role in the company.

Answering Questions

While being relaxed can be a huge advantage during an interview it can also cause you problems as well. Be on guard as you answer questions trying to answer each one as completely as possible without saying too much at the same time. In other words, give them full and complete answers to every question and then stop talking. No small talk and no personal stories except for be sociable and nice to the interviewer.

A lot of interviewers will ask you questions designed to get you to talk and volunteer information you otherwise would keep to yourself. Be relaxed but be guarded and careful at the same time. That is another reason why practicing answers to the most common questions will help you answer questions without providing too much extra information.

Stay on Message

If you have done your homeowner you probably will have a message and a game plan in mind when you sit down for the interview. Try to stick with that plan and approach and do not give mixed or conflicting signals. Unless you see that your original approach is clearly not working, stay on point and try to return the conversation back to where it was previously going.

If you start out with one focus and change it in mid-stream the interviewer is going to wonder if you are sincere or just telling them what you think they want to hear. You want to stay on point, establish your credibility and keep your message and your focus intact throughout the entire interview.

Limit Small Talk

You want to remain friendly but watch small talk at the same time. A skilled and experienced interviewer will know how to steer the conversation around to get you to release personal information or information that you otherwise might have kept to yourself. Keep small talk to a minimum but remain friendly and engaging at the same time.

As we have already said, stay away from politics, religion and other polarizing subjects as well as off color or ethnic humor. Sometimes what you say and what you talk about can provide a real insight into who you really are. Think twice before you speak and if there are any doubts, don't say it. It is better to be safe than uncertain.

Conclusion

Having read through every step of preparing to crush a job interview and annihilate your competitors, what remains are the practical bits and bytes of it. Are you going to keep employing the same old tricks that have seen you hunt for a job for years on end, or are you going to implement this useful e-book to help you land a job in your next interview? Your guess is as good as mine, but a step-by-step implementation of this e-book is the ultimate path to crushing a job interview. It might not take a day, but with consistent practice, it will ultimately prove its worth.

CPSIA information can be obtained
at www.ICGtesting.com
Printed in the USA
BVHW062023310820
587704BV00015B/278